WRITERS AND THEIR WORK

ISOBEL ARMSTRONG
Consultant Editor

PRE-RAPHAELITISM:
POETRY AND PAINTING

PRE-RAPHAELITISM:
POETRY AND PAINTING

Lindsay Smith

NORTHCOTE

BRITISH COUNCIL

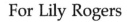

For Lily Rogers

© Copyright 2013 by Lindsay Smith

First published in 2013 by Northcote House Publishers Ltd, Horndon House, Horndon, Tavistock, Devon, PL19 9NQ, United Kingdom. Tel: +44 (0) 1822 810066 Fax: +44 (0) 1822 810034.

British Library Cataloguing-in-Publication Data
A catalogue record for this book is available from the British Library

ISBN 978-0-7463-0806-6 hardcover
ISBN 978-0-7463-0805-9 paperback

Typeset by PDQ Typesetting, Newcastle-under-Lyme
Printed and bound by CPI Group (UK) Ltd, Croydon, CR0 4YY

Contents

Acknowledgements		vii
Timeline		viii
Abbreviations and References		xii
List of Plates		xiv
Preamble		1
Introduction		4
1	One tiny calf-bound volume	26
2	Several dead women and one dead man	34
3	*Ut Pictura Poesis*: early Pre-Raphaelite poetry and the case of *The Germ*	45
4	Dante Gabriel Rossetti's 'paired works'	65
5	'The Fleshly School' Controversy	75
6	Dante's *La Vita Nuova*	94
7	The Shade	100
Afterthought		117
Notes		120
Select Bibliography		128
Index		134

Acknowledgements

My thanks to the Aberdeen Art Gallery and Museums Collection, Leighton House Museum, London, the Russell-Cotes Art Gallery and Museum, Bournemouth, and the Tate Britain, London for kind permission to reproduce paintings in their collections. I would also like to thank the Rossetti Archive for allowing me to cite Dante Gabriel Rossetti's 'Unburied Love' and 'Another Love'. I am grateful to Isobel Armstrong for originally commissioning this book and to Brian Hulme and staff at Northcote House Publishers for bringing it out.

Timeline

1842   Turner paints *The Blue Rigi* in Switzerland and *Snow Storm – Steam Boat off a Harbour's Mouth*. Ruskin commissions his first watercolours from Turner.

1843   Publication of Ruskin's *Modern Painters I*.

1844   Hunt, Millais and Stephens meet at Royal Academy Schools.

1845   D. G. Rossetti enters RA Schools.

1846   Ruskin publishes *Modern Painters II*; Rossetti reads *Modern Painters*. Millais exhibits first work at RA.

1847   Holman-Hunt reads *Modern Painters*.

1848   Pre-Raphaelite Brotherhood founded. Members: W. Holman Hunt, J. E. Millais, D. G. Rossetti, W. M. Rossetti, T. Woolner, J. Collinson and F. G. Stephens. D. G. Rossetti writes 'Unburied Death'. Ruskin and Effie Gray marry at Bowerswell, near Perth. Christina Rossetti becomes engaged to Collinson but engagement broken off owing to his Catholicism.

1849   First paintings exhibited with the insignia PRB including D. G. Rossetti's *The Girlhood of Mary Virgin*, Millais' *Isabella* and Hunt's *Rienzi*. Rossetti and Hunt visit Paris, Belgium and Holland. Ruskin publishes *The Seven Lamps of Architecture*.

1850   Pre-Raphaelite journal *The Germ* founded. D.G. Rossetti's 'My Sister's Sleep' and Christina Rossetti's 'Dream Land' appear in the first issue. Ruskin sees Pre-Raphaelite works at RA exhibition including Millais' *Christ in the House of his Parents*, Millais' *Mariana* and C. Collins' *Convent Thoughts*. Tennyson publishes *In Memoriam* and becomes Poet Laureate following Wordsworth's death.

1851   Ruskin writes to *The Times* in defence of the Pre-Raphaelites and publishes the pamphlet *Pre-Raphaelitism* and *The Stones of Venice* volume I. Millais paints the riverbank in Ewell for *Ophelia*. Death of J. M. W. Turner; Great Exhibition of the Industry of all Nations at the Crystal Palace, Hyde Park.

1852   Woolner emigrates to Australia. Christina Rossetti writes the sonnet 'PRB'. Ford Madox Brown paints *The Last of England*. Théophile Gautier publishes *Emaux et Camées*.

1853   Millais paints Ruskin's portrait in Scotland at Glenfinlas. Ruskin publishes *The Stones of Venice* II and III. William Morris and Edward Burne Jones meet at Oxford.

1854   Ruskin's marriage to Effie Gray breaks up. Rossetti meets Ruskin. Hunt leaves for the Holy Land and exhibits *The Light of the World* and *The Awakening Conscience* at the RA.

1855   Ruskin begins to act as patron of Elizabeth Siddal. Millais marries Effie Gray following the annulment on the grounds of non-consummation of her marriage to Ruskin.

1856   Ruskin publishes *Modern Painters III* (January) and *Modern Painters IV* (April). D.G.Rossetti's 'The Woodspurge'. Henry Wallis' *The Death of Chatterton*; Swinburne enters Balliol College, Oxford.

1857   Ford Madox Brown organizes Pre-Raphaelite exhibition at 4 Russell Place. Rossetti, Hughes, Morris, Burne-Jones, Prinsep paint the Oxford Union murals. Wallis' *Chatterton* exhibited at the Manchester Art Treasures Exhibition. Moxon's edition of Tennyson's *Poems* published with illustrations by Rossetti, Hunt and Millais. Baudelaire publishes *Les Fleurs du mal*; John Brett paints *The Stonebreaker* (1857–8).

1858   Morris publishes *The Defence of Guenevere and Other Poems*. Simeon Solomon exhibits at the RA for the first time. Henry Peach Robinson exhibits *Fading Away*. Ruskin meets Rose La Touche.

1859   Morris marries Jane Burden and they move to Red House, Bexleyheath designed by Philip Webb. Rossetti's *Bocca Baciata*.

1860	Marriage of D. G. Rossetti and Elizabeth Siddal. Ruskin publishes *Modern Painters V* and the first instalment of *Unto This Last* in *The Cornhill Magazine*.
1861	D. G. Rossetti publishes *Early Italian Poets* (including his translation of Dante's *La Vita Nuova*); Morris, Marshall, Faulkner and Co. founded. Elizabeth Siddal gives birth to a stillborn daughter.
1862	Death of Elizabeth Siddal from an overdose of laudanum. Christina Rossetti publishes *Goblin Market and Other Poems*; Swinburne publishes poetry and essays in the *Spectator* including his review of Baudelaire's *Les Fleurs du mal*.
1863	Millais elected Royal Academician.
1864	D. G. Rossetti paints *Beata Beatrix*, *Venus Verticordia* (1864–8). Frederic Leighton exhibits *Orpheus and Eurydice* accompanied by Robert Browning's poem 'Eurydice to Orpheus'.
1865	D. G. Rossetti's *The Blue Bower*; Ruskin publishes *Sesame and Lilies*.
1866	Swinburne publishes *Poems and Ballads*; John Morley's review of Swinburne appears in *The Saturday Review*. Christina Rossetti publishes *The Prince's Progress*.
1867	Ruskin delivers lecture on 'The Relation of National Ethics to National Arts' at the Senate House, Cambridge.
1868	Morris publishes *The Earthly Paradise*.
1869	Disinterment of Siddal's grave to retrieve Rossetti's manuscript book of poems. Ruskin elected first Slade Professor of Fine Art at Oxford. Solomon's *Sacramentum Amoris* exhibited at the Fifth General Exhibition of Water-Colour drawings, Dudley Gallery.
1870	D. G. Rossetti publishes *Poems*.
1871	Thomas Buchanan publishes 'The Fleshly School of Poetry' in *The Contemporary Review*. Swinburne publishes *Songs before Sunrise*. D. G. Rossetti publishes his response to Buchanan's attack 'The Stealthy School of Criticism' in *The Atheneaum*. Solomon publishes *A Vision of Love Revealed in Sleep*. Rossetti completes *Dante's Dream of the Death of Beatrice*. Ruskin begins the serial publication of *Fors Clavigera, Letters to the Workmen and Labourers of Great Britain*.

1872	Swinburne replies to Buchanan's attack in *Under the Microscope*. Christina Rossetti publishes *Sing Song. A Nursery Rhyme Book*. George Frederic Watts' *Orpheus and Eurydice* (1872–7). D. G. Rossetti suffers a mental and emotional breakdown.
1873	Solomon arrested for 'buggery' in a public place. Walter Pater publishes *Studies in the History of the Renaissance*.
1874	Rossetti begins *Proserpine*, modelled on Jane Morris. G. F. Watts' *Love and Death* (1874–7).
1875	Death of Rose La Touche. Rossetti's *Astarte Syriaca* (1875–7).
1876	Ruskin suffers onset of mental instability.
1877	Opening of the Grosvenor Gallery, London. Ruskin writes his attack on Whistler's pictures in the first exhibition there (*Fors Clavigera* no.79).
1878	Ruskin-Whistler trial. Ruskin suffers mental illness. Frederic Leighton elected President of the Royal Academy.

Abbreviations and References

Armstrong   Isobel Armstrong, *Victorian Poetry: Poetry, Poetics and Politics* (London: Routledge, 1993)

Blanchot   Maurice Blanchot, *The Gaze of Orpheus and Other Literary Essays*, trans. Lydia Davis (New York: Station Hill Press, 1981)

Bronfen   Elizabeth Bronfen, *Over her Dead Body, Death, Femininity and the Aesthetic* (Manchester: Manchester University Press, 1992)

Buchanan   Thomas Maitland, (Thomas Buchanan), 'The Fleshly School of Poetry' *Contemporary Review* October 1871

Diaries   *The Diaries of John Ruskin*, eds. Joan Evans and John Howard Whitehouse (Oxford: Oxford University Press, 1956) 2 vols

DW   *The Letters of Dante Gabriel Rossetti* eds. O. Doughty and J. R. Wall (1965–1967) 4 vols

Gadamer   Hans-Georg Gadamer, 'Poetry and Mimesis', in *The Relevance of the Beautiful and Other Essays* (Cambridge: CUP, 1986)

Germ   *The Germ: Thoughts towards Nature in Poetry, Literature, and Art* issues 1–2 (London, Aylott & Jones, 1850). After the first two numbers: *Art and Poetry: Thoughts towards Nature Conducted principally by Artists*

Hagstrum   Jean Hagstrum, *The Sister Arts: The Tradition of Literary Pictorialism and English Poetry From Dryden to Gray* (Chicago: University of Chicago Press, 1958)

Marsh   Jan Marsh, *Dante Gabriel Rossetti Painter and Poet* (London: Weidenfeld & Nicolson, 1999)

Michie   Helena Michie, *Victorian Honeymoons: Journeys to the Conjugal* (Cambridge: Cambridge University Press, 2006)

Prosser   Jay Prosser, *Light in the Dark Room: Photography and Loss* (Minneapolis: University of Minnesota Press, 2005)

RA   *Rossetti Archive*, Jerome McGann, *The Complete Writings and Pictures of Dante Gabriel Rossetti; a Hypermedia Archive*, http://www.rossettiarchive.org (2000)

Ruskin   *The Complete Works of John Ruskin* (Library Edition), eds. E. T. Cook and Alexander Wedderburn, 39 vols. (London: George Allen, 1903–12)

Smith   Lindsay Smith, *Victorian Photography, Painting and Poetry: The Enigma of Visibility in Ruskin, Morris and the Pre-Raphaelites* (Cambridge: Cambridge University Press, 1995)

VN   D. G. Rossetti, *The Vita Nuova*, in Jan Marsh, *Dante Gabriel Rossetti: Collected Writings* (Chicago: New Amsterdam Books, 2000), 76–128

List of Plates

Cover   Dante Gabriel Rossetti, *Venus Verticordia*
(1864–8) Russell-Cotes Museum and Art Gallery

1.   John Everett Millais, *Ophelia* (1851–2) Tate Britain   35

2.   Henry Wallis, *The Death of Chatterton* (1855–6)
Tate Britain   37

3.   Dante Gabriel Rossetti, *Proserpine* (1874)
Tate Britain   102

4.   Frederic Leighton, *Orpheus and Eurydice* (1864)
Leighton House Museum   106

5.   George Frederic Watts, *Orpheus and Eurydice*
(1869) Aberdeen Art Gallery and Museums
Collection   109

Preamble

The question as to who in the nineteenth century may qualify as a Pre-Raphaelite remains a contested one. But it is not the project of this book to settle that question or to come up with a new catalogue of Pre-Raphaelite poets. At issue, rather, is what we might term a Pre-Raphaelite aesthetic, present in the work of a number of poets and painters and in several cases one that extended beyond a 'first' or 'second' generation of writers and artists. Faithful to the nature and scope of this series I have chosen to re-think Pre-Raphaelite poetry, beginning with its relation to the work of Ruskin, principally through the figures of Christina Rossetti, Dante Gabriel Rossetti, Algernon Charles Swinburne, and Simeon Solomon. Of these, D. G. Rossetti gets the most page-time by virtue of the fact that not only was he a key founder member of the Pre-Raphaelite Brotherhood, and a magnetic personality around whom other artists and writers clustered, but also because more than any other figure he newly focused the interrelationship of poetry and painting, a take on the sister-arts analogy, that remains the most innovative and enabling legacy of the movement.

While it may not have been novel in the nineteenth century to twin a poem with a picture, or to aspire to work in the dual realms of language and paint, the Pre-Raphaelites took up the correspondence between visual and verbal, revising the sister-arts analogy to new aesthetic and political ends. By the same token, Ruskin and D. G. Rossetti may not immediately strike us as a likely, or sympathetic, pairing (Ruskin reputedly fastidious, abstemious; Rossetti: bohemian, indulgent) but Ruskin supported Rossetti at a vital time in his career, recognizing that his unusual talent did not lie chiefly in the sphere of artistic technique in which he was surpassed by John Everett Millais

1

and William Holman Hunt. In his links with Rossetti, Ruskin also realized a profound psychological connection through love and loss, through mourning and a desire for resurrection. These motives haunt both men and underpin aspects of Pre-Raphaelitism that morphed into those subsequently recognizably Symbolist creations of Walter Pater and Oscar Wilde.

As early as 1852 Christina Rossetti's sonnet 'The P.R.B.' crystallizes that sense of brevity that marked the existence of the Pre-Raphaelite Brotherhood as a group. But Rossetti's poem also contains the grain of prophecy, the sense of forward reach implicit in the movement that this book will be continually drawn back to:

> The P. R. B. is in its decadence:
> For Woolner in Australia cooks his chops,
> And Hunt is yearning for the land of Cheops;
> D. G. Rossetti shuns the vulgar optic;
> While William M. Rossetti merely lops
> His B's in English disesteemed as Coptic;
> Calm Stephens in the twilight smokes his pipe,
> But long the dawning of his public day;
> And he at last, the champion, great Millais,
> Attaining academic opulence,
> Winds up his signature with A. R. A.
> So rivers merge in the perpetual sea,
> So luscious fruit must fall when overripe,
> And so the consummated P. R. B.

Demonstrating her engagement with Pre-Raphaelite artists and writers, Rossetti's witty pronouncement that the PRB is in its decadence after a mere four years also records the artists' dispersal to various geographic locations: by 1852 Thomas Woolner had indeed emigrated to Australia while William Holman Hunt increasingly 'yearn[ed] for the land of Cheops' and, two years later, was to paint the Great Pyramid at Giza commissioned by that Egyptian Pharaoh in the 27 Century BC. Nonetheless, his initial reaction as recorded in a letter to Millais (16 March 1854) attests to the fact that, except for the palm trees, 'one might as well sketch in Hackney Marsh.'[1] John Everett Millais, meanwhile, would be elected in 1853 an Associate Royal Academician, thereafter 'wind [ing] up his signature' with that acronym of which Rossetti here discloses prior knowledge. The

2

sonnet is affectionately dismissive with the sprung rhyme of 'chops' with 'Cheops' at the ends of the second and third lines introducing a tone of familiarity with the individual artists portrayed. Moreover, Rossetti distinguishes between the 'vulgar' and by definition what must constitute a non-vulgar 'optic' as practised by her brother Dante Gabriel. Brother number two, William Michael, meanwhile 'merely lops his B's' and, along with 'calm Stephens' seems disinclined to fame. The final couplet – 'So luscious fruit must fall when overripe;/ and so the consummated P.R.B' – plays interestingly upon fruition; a sense of the group having attained its artistic ends following on from the idea that early distinctiveness must inevitably become incorporated into the 'perpetual sea' of a wider public domain.

Powerfully conveying the extremity of a premature 'decadence' the sonnet is additionally ironic in its affectionate failure to predict the far-reaching aesthetic momentum of the group that would continue long after the 'fall' of such 'overripe' fruit. Yet, in another sense, the verse perfectly encapsulates that odd temporal drive of the movement: the 'always too late' – the harking back as encased in the 'pre' of Pre-Raphaelite. Indeed, as we shall find, while Pre-Raphaelite poems and paintings anticipate life, that life, as it were, subsequently unfolds to re-invest the artworks with additional and peculiar forms of prophecy.

Introduction

September 12th. BADEN. Scenery rather finish, pretty hills, and fine views of the Alps, the same almost as, only more distant than, that of Rigi, who rises below them very black or blue or a sort of hobbletehoy between-colour. John Ruskin, diary entry 1835 (*Diaries* I, 60).

On 2 March 2007 *The Guardian* newspaper reported the saving by the Tate Gallery and the British public of Joseph Mallord William Turner's 'The Blue Rigi'.[1] Painted in Switzerland in 1842 the small late watercolour, one in a series of three depicting the mountain from the shore of Lake Lucerne, was about to be lost to a foreign buyer. But thanks to a heritage lottery grant, a pledge from the Tate itself, and the generous donations of individuals, the required 4.95 million pounds was raised to maintain the unassuming national 'treasure'. While the work now remains in public hands in the UK, Turner's companion paintings 'The Red' and 'The Dark Rigi', depicting different atmospheric conditions of the same prospect, will continue to belong respectively to the National Gallery of Melbourne and a private UK collector. As the fate of 'The Blue Rigi' demonstrates, the singular legacy of Turner is today without doubt; the aesthetic and material worth of his relatively modest-sized works on paper are largely unchallenged. But for the celebrated nineteenth century art critic and theorist John Ruskin, however, this scenario would have been quite different. By a curious clairvoyance Ruskin's diary entry, made seven years before Turner's painting, visualizes for us in advance 'The Blue Rigi' with its 'hobbletehoy'-coloured mountain. Yet, still the ongoing battle Ruskin fought during his lifetime to ensure enduring critical appreciation of Turner's work remains easily overlooked.

4

So too does the significance of Ruskin's support for the Pre-Raphaelites, that legendary group of initially seven painters and writers: John Everett Millais, William Holman Hunt, Dante Gabriel Rossetti, William Michael Rossetti, Thomas Woolner, James Collinson and Frederic George Stephens, who established a brotherhood in London in 1848.

Though by no means on the same scale as his championing of Turner, Ruskin's support for the Pre-Raphaelites in letters to *The Times* in the early 1850s is on a continuum with his well-known defence of the artist. Indeed, Ruskin's desire to make intelligible to a confounded public the works of the young British painters arose from the case he had already made for Turner's having essentially re-conceptualized the relationship between visual perception and representation. Like Turner, Pre-Raphaelite painters represented the potential for a revolutionary national style. Moreover, Ruskin celebrates Turner's physical marks of paint as aspiring to that visual condition which they themselves describe. Thus, paintings by Turner, such as 'The Blue Rigi', now remain precious to the nation in large part owing to their commemoration (or what Proust referred to in a different context as 'resurrection') in Ruskin's prose. By the same token, though by different method, in his much cited 'Letter to *The Times*' 13 May 1851, Ruskin was the first to translate to a bemused public the value of the hallucinatory realism of the surfaces of Charles Collins' *Convent Thoughts* (1851) and John Everett Millais' *Mariana* (1850). Even though dismissive of elements of both paintings for what he called 'their Romanist and Tractarian tendencies' – Collins' novice and Mariana's 'painted window and idolatrous toilet table' – Ruskin praised Collins' water-plant for enabling him to match it to its Latin name *Alisma Plantago*. He likewise singled out as the most 'earnest' and 'complete' in art 'since the days of Albert Durer,' 'the white draperies in the table' of *Mariana* together with minor details of other Pre-Raphaelite canvases (*Ruskin* XII, 323). More emphatically, Ruskin recognized as largely unprecedented the brilliant colouring and intense realism of Millais' canvas. Indeed, although ideally embodied for him in Turner's painting, what Ruskin identified as a new relationship between visual perception and representation went far beyond the work of a single artist. For a Pre-Raphaelite commitment to the physiological

5

conditions of seeing signalled equally for Ruskin a condition of modernity in its most radical phenomenological embodiment.

While we tend to consider the work of the Pre-Raphaelites as having been largely visual, I hope to demonstrate that it was equally intensely verbal. More emphatically, Pre-Raphaelite artists and writers came together initially to work creatively on the intersections of image and text, opening up new ways of thinking about the material and the metaphysical qualities of both paint and language. Undoubtedly, a seemingly incompatible mix of Pre-Raphaelite realism and extreme symbolism has continued to perplex critics, but the story that such an odd synthesis may tell retrospectively is one excitingly rooted in contemporary nineteenth-century developments in a range of aesthetic, social and scientific discourses. These came together to redefine mid-nineteenth century understanding of processes of seeing and visualizing the world. Moreover, although historically the term 'Pre-Raphaelite' remains a rather approximate one, we might turn to our advantage the very looseness of the category to designate most crucially both a poetry and painting reluctant to separate visual from verbal. For, as this book contends, the perpetually hesitant quality of the term 'Pre-Raphaelite', with its prepositional construction opening up a vast previous realm of all that came before Raphael (1483–1520), might best signal the concerns of Victorian writers and painters who engaged the historically difficult and ineffable relationship of word and image. Indeed, among the literary outputs of Pre-Raphaelitism, we may distinguish between poetry premised upon an understanding, albeit half-formulated, of principles advocated by an artistically naïve brotherhood of painters, and poetry written later and only retrospectively attributed to the category 'Pre-Raphaelite'. The same is true of the visual works. For some, the term 'Pre-Raphaelite' only applies to visual art produced within the comparatively brief period of the artists' existence as a self-consciously constituted group, while for others the epithet extends from 1848 as far as the end of the century, exemplified by painters such as William Waterhouse for whom Tennyson's 'Lady of Shalott' remained a favourite subject.

While the present study explores aspects of a Pre-Raphaelite aesthetic both in its emergent and some of its later phases, it does so by a self-consciously inverted chronology. Thereby, after first detailing the importance to those artists and poets of Ruskin's work, it immediately ranges forward to 1869 to the case of D. G. Rossetti's 'lost' and 'found' poems; that is the occasion upon which Elizabeth Siddal's body was exhumed from Highgate Cemetery in order that Rossetti might retrieve a manuscript book of poetry he had buried with her seven years before. I begin with that notorious occasion in order to demonstrate ways in which the troubled history of what would constitute Rossetti's *Poems* of 1870, their journey to the grave and back, came to affect not only works that followed them, but also retrospectively those, including the collective project of the periodical *The Germ*, which came before. For, it is only by fundamentally re-considering what it might have meant in 1869 to exhume a volume of poems, and the investment in an act of resurrection, that we may come to understand those specific ways in which Pre-Raphaelitism as a movement uniquely engaged visual and verbal forms of representation.

STARTING WITH RUSKIN

Most studies of the Pre-Raphaelites have emerged squarely from within the domain of Art History. This circumstance is perhaps not surprising since the artists' 'manifesto', with an emphasis upon working directly from 'nature' and restoring to painting purity of colour, was most concerned with reforming fine art practices rather than literary ones. Although there have been some key discussions of Pre-Raphaelitism within literary criticism, such as the seminal study by Lionel Stevenson, few have attempted to unlock the inter-disciplinary project of the group.[2] Elizabeth Helsinger's recent study is an exception here, taking up the visual and verbal in D. G. Rossetti and William Morris.[3] Apart from my *Victorian Photography, Painting and Poetry* (1995) none has assumed as a sustained point of departure Ruskin's influence upon the painters and writers. Ruskin published the first volume of *Modern Painters* in 1843. And from that date until 1889 when he composed the last fragments of his autobiography *Praeterita* Ruskin produced a vast number of works pioneering in their inter-disciplinary scope. Exploring many creative fields in addition to that of painting Ruskin's singular aesthetic theory fundamentally altered the relationship of the visual arts to other art forms in the period. Moreover, it brought to the fore the social basis of painting as rooted in its historical and political context. Relatively early in its formation the Pre-Raphaelite Brotherhood received the public support of Ruskin.

When their paintings were first exhibited in 1849 (D. G. Rossetti's *The Girlhood of Mary Virgin* at the Free Institution, Hyde Park Corner, and Millais' *Isabella* and Hunt's *Rienzi* at the Royal Academy, London) they were well-received critically. Reviewers praised the technique and characterization of Millais' painting and Bulwer Lytton upon whose novel *Rienzi* Hunt's painting was based, praised the work as 'full of genius – & high promise', while Rossetti's painting sold for eighty guineas to a family acquaintance, the Dowager Marchioness of Bath. But, the following year, once rumour had spread that the collective insignia 'PRB' appearing on the artists' paintings in place of individual signatures represented a secret society, the Pre-Raphaelites attracted negative attention. Thus, when in 1850 Rossetti exhibited at the Portland Gallery a second painting of the Virgin entitled *Ecce Ancilla Domini!* (*The Annunciation*) and Millais and Holman Hunt showed at the Royal Academy respectively *Christ in the House of his Parents* and *A Converted British Family Sheltering a Christian Missionary from the Persecution of the Druids*, the young artists were stung by the hostile response they received. In particular the extreme critical wrath of such a prominent public figure as the novelist Charles Dickens who claimed that Millais' painting represented 'the lowest depths of what [was] mean, odious, repulsive and revolting' threatened to undermine the larger philosophical ideals of the group.[4] In response, Ruskin defended the young painters in judicial letters to *The Times* newspaper. Rather in the manner in which he had earlier begun his defence of Turner, when during the 1840s the artist had been vilified for what Ruskin regarded as the unique modernity of his paintings, Ruskin was impelled to defend what he believed to be the singular method and vision of works by Millais and Holman Hunt.

Turner was without doubt, as Ruskin so uniquely demonstrated, a visionary in the vanguard of painting the constituents of visual perception itself, and, being the first to recognize the significance of that vision, Ruskin would continue to defend the painter unequivocally. Some might say he went too far too soon, crafting a defence in excess of the prosecution, but in the case of the Pre-Raphaelites Ruskin was more circumspect. Having little prior knowledge of the individual artists, he took care, for example, to separate himself from what had been perceived by some as Catholic tendencies in their works. At the same time, however, in defending Pre-Raphaelite paintings Ruskin recognized in what were stylistically very different canvases significant connections to the earlier work of Turner. Indeed, aspects of a Pre-Raphaelite aesthetic as Ruskin interpreted it might take up where Turner had left off. For in spite of their dissimilar artistic styles one fundamental connection emerged in the peculiar quality of 'modernity' in their paintings.

Referring in his 'Letter to *The Times*' 30 May 1851 to Millais' rendering of detail in his painting *The Return of the Dove to the Ark*, Ruskin notes that the hay is 'painted not only elaborately but with the most perfect ease of touch and mastery of effect especially to be observed because this freedom of execution is a modern excellence and a distinguishing quality of Pre-Raphaelite painting' (*Ruskin* XII, 326). Ruskin's stress upon 'freedom of execution' as denoting a peculiarly 'modern excellence' discloses the extent to which he regarded the young painters as stylistic pioneers of a new philosophy of art, the aesthetic basis of which required an intricate balancing of visual and verbal. Moreover, in further support of the artists' careers, in 1856 Ruskin followed his letters to *The Times* supporting the Pre-Raphaelites with a pamphlet entitled *Pre-Raphaelitism*. Around the same time, he also began to write an annual 'circular letter' entitled *Academy Notes* in which he commented on pictures in the Academy exhibitions. The first of five parts was issued in 1855 and, designed to further the Pre-Raphaelite cause, the notes directly encouraged those artists in the Royal Academy exhibitions who adhered to Pre-Raphaelite principles. While it is clear that Ruskin's 'defence' of the Pre-Raphaelites was not based upon any obvious personal gain, his motives for supporting the artists represented at once an attempt to lend them encouragement at a formative time in their development and also, though more indirectly, a means of extending his defence of Turner's work:

9

what he believed Turner's painting to represent uniquely in contemporary British art.

This study demonstrates that it is only in such a context of Ruskin's profound impact upon the movement that an understanding of the verbal and visual, together with the historical and theoretical tenets of Pre-Raphaelitism, emerges. For the Pre-Raphaelites painting and poetry make little sense in isolation or as essentially discrete categories. As a consequence, in order to understand their poetic and painterly outputs it is necessary to reconsider ways in which both Pre-Raphaelite verbal and visual practices quickly gathered momentum, extending far beyond the conception of the original brotherhood of artists. Ruskin's influence is fundamental in this respect. Considering the dependency of the movement upon a pairing of painting and poetry, his writings become especially pivotal to an understanding of Pre-Raphaelite painters' and poets' desire to explore intersections between the contemporary physical world and its seeming antithesis: the abstruse metaphysical realm.

Yet the nature of Ruskin's influence upon the original Pre-Raphaelite grouping of 1848 remains a contentious topic. In what represents a curious desire for disassociation, William Michael Rossetti, brother of the poets Christina and Dante Gabriel Rossetti, early on turned readers' attentions away from any possible impact upon the Pre-Raphaelites of Ruskin's work. Indeed, he claimed that none of the initial brotherhood apart from William Holman Hunt had any knowledge of Ruskin. This act of deflection is all the more curious when we know, as Jan Marsh reminds us, that D. G. Rossetti was avidly reading *Modern Painters II* when it came out in 1846. While some, following W. M. Rossetti's lead, remain sceptical of any profound influence of Ruskin upon the initial creative output of the Pre-Raphaelites, arguing that the group of painters was too immature and ill read in Ruskin's work to have received any determinate aesthetic influence from him, others articulate only in passing a connection between a 'Pre-Raphaelite' visual imperative and Ruskin's writing. What is certain is that in line with W. M. Rossetti's account there has remained a tendency to minimize the importance to the movement of Ruskin's influence. In order to address this relative neglect we have to consider afresh Ruskin's desire to encompass so many areas of social and

10

aesthetic debate, not as the peculiar expression of an eccentric genius, but as a culturally specific desire to question boundaries between discrete disciplines. Focusing in particular upon historically determined distinctions between visual and verbal modes of representation, we must reassess Ruskin's impact upon Pre-Raphaelite writers and artists for whom the age-old sister arts analogy of *ut pictura poesis* ('as a painting, so also a poem') was ripe for significant revision. As we shall find, the Pre-Raphaelites are fascinated by transitional states that articulate a pared-down relation between word and image.

To reinstate both the scope and specificity of Ruskin's influence allows us to consider a Pre-Raphaelite aesthetic as a contingent category in the process of its formulation. Indeed, during the early 1850s Pre-Raphaelitism did not occupy the assured position we now attribute to it; Ruskin's work encourages us to reassess the movement in terms of its discontinuities without immediately over-simplifying and making regular what are enabling inconsistencies in the early work. However, since Ruskin himself created a huge corpus readers might be deterred by the sheer volume of material from ever finding a clear channel by which to navigate the thirty-nine volumes of the *Collected Works*, or their more recent CD Rom incarnation. For, in addition to writing, Ruskin produced drawings and paintings. He collected and catalogued. He diarized, wrote letters and made intricate notebooks. In each of these contexts, in themselves never divorced from his more instantly recognizable spheres of theorizing, his aesthetic preoccupations evolved by way of fascinating and frequently tenuous connections. Yet, it is important to remember that, in first coming to Ruskin in the late 1840s, the Pre-Raphaelites were not faced with the daunting editorial feat of Cook and Wedderburn. There did not exist for those young artists the difficulty of extricating the first books of *Modern Painters* from subsequent ones. Those first books of *Modern Painters* initially were all they had and the Pre-Raphaelites took them up with a passion and an aesthetic conviction difficult to recreate in retrospect.

Equally, but differently, for us as readers of Ruskin today it is tempting to fix upon a single aspect of his art theory and to forgo a range of those intellectual enquiries that comprise a complex and integrated aesthetic. Similarly, we might find

Ruskin's morality a barrier at odds with some of the creative work he was defending. Certainly his moral investment in art has been, and remains, a sticking point for a number of critics. But Ruskin engaged a political project. He was convinced that contemporary British painting was in a state of decline and had the foresight not only to recognize, but also to forcefully articulate, Turner's radicalism long before anyone else had paid much attention to the painter's uncompromisingly abstract canvases. It is for this reason in part that we may detect a profound irony in the infamous Ruskin/Whistler trial of November 1878 for the extreme moralistic light in which it invariably cast Ruskin. A year before the trial, Ruskin had published an attack on James McNeil Whistler's painting *Nocturne in Black and Gold: the Falling Rocket* (1875) displayed at the new Grosvenor Gallery in London. Ruskin wrote in *Fors Clavigera*:

> the eccentricities of such art are always in some degree forced; and their imperfections gratuitously, if not impertinently indulged. [....] I have seen, and heard much of Cockney impudence before now; but never expected to hear a coxcomb ask two hundred guineas for flinging a pot of paint in the public's face. (*Ruskin* XXIV, 160)

As the outcome of that episode in art history demonstrates (Whistler sued Ruskin for £1000 in damages for libel, Ruskin lost and was ordered to pay one farthing without costs in contemptuous damages to Whistler), it is all too easy to forget the theoretical and political nuances of Ruskin's legacy and cast him as an enemy of 'art for art's sake'. Indeed, in many ways the trial diverted attention from very complex and more general issues pertaining to visual representation. On the surface of things, Whistler triumphed from the episode as a proto-modernist, an unproblematic supporter of Post-Impressionism, while Ruskin came across as a moralizer subject to severe mental lapses. But as Adam Parkes has recently pointed out, that trial, always dismissed on account of the extreme absurdity of Ruskin's accusation against Whistler, raises profound points about those ways in which 'the apparently opposed aesthetics of artist and critic overlap in significant ways'.[5] Whistler's notion that a painting communicates through sensation was not absolutely antithetical to Ruskin's beliefs but where the two diverged most markedly was on the role of the critic where Whistler's 'individualism threatened to undermine Ruskin's entire cultural endeavour': 'in Ruskin's view, critics performed a vital task because, in enabling spectators to appreciate art, they created the conditions for widespread involvement in a larger cultural conversation, which would form the basis of an authentic moral community'. [6] Following suit the Pre-Raphaelites instigated new forms of cultural conversation.

Ruskin's 'cultural endeavour', which had at its centre a commitment to establishing the political, social and intellectual conditions for a 'larger cultural conversation' to take place, drove his approach to art. But such a project did not prevent him from embracing work in relation with which he encountered 'moral' difficulties. Indeed, in terms of artistic tolerance, we should recall, in the context of the Whistler trial, that when earlier in 1866 so many reviewers were deeming Algernon Charles Swinburne's poetry outrageous – for its sexual content and its obvious indebtedness to the French authors Victor Hugo (1802–85) and Charles Baudelaire (1821–67) – Ruskin recognized, and was willing to speak of, its unique power, even though he personally wished Swinburne would turn his attention to what he regarded as more felicitous subject matter. In other words, Ruskin was able to separate his own moral position from an appreciation of Swinburne's poetic language. While, clearly Ruskin's desire for art as 'a noble and expressive language' might suggest rather limited political scope, it would be wrong to accept a strict polarity between the aesthetic and the moral in Ruskin's work. For his early texts comprise a sustained critique of the establishment of British painting just as his later ones make an important intervention in the field of political economy. Moreover, Ruskin's critique of the alienation of the British factory worker in the celebrated 'Nature of Gothic' chapter from *The Stones of Venice* (1851–3) preceded that of Karl Marx, while his troublingly unorthodox essays on political economy published in *The Cornhill Magazine* and subsequently as *Unto This Last* prompted the editor to suppress an intended fourth piece for fear of its disturbing radicalism. It would be thereby inappropriate to take the Ruskin of the late 1870s as representative of the Ruskin with whom the Pre-Raphaelites identified in the 1850s, for huge changes take place in the interim.

13

Undoubtedly, Ruskin did more than simply inspire and champion the young and inexperienced artists of the brotherhood. He also provided a hospitable intellectual context in which their work might be received. Yet, for many, such support remains at odds with his support for Turner; there appears little congruity between Ruskin's predilection for both Turner and the Pre-Raphaelites. Put most simply: how might Ruskin the great Victorian sage have found the paintings of William Holman Hunt, Dante Gabriel Rossetti, and John Everett Millais, together with those of Turner, similarly remarkable for their optical fidelity, for the close attention to natural detail or, to use Ruskin's celebrated phrase, for their 'truth to nature'? How might Ruskin see fit to conceptualize links between artistic methods that in formal terms appear to be so far apart? In the context of recent re-evaluations of Pre-Raphaelite works such questions remain pertinent to accounts of vision especially in the sense of the relationship of the empirical to the transcendental. The present study takes up such questions of vision in Pre-Raphaelite poetry as well as painting. In so doing, it makes claims for a distinctive Pre-Raphaelite aesthetic within a diversity of artistic and poetic purposes and practices.

From their position of aspiring artists interested in exploring, if only to begin with in thought, a new national style based on a critique of the Royal Academy, the institution at which they were receiving their training, the Pre-Raphaelites began interpreting Ruskin precisely at that time when he himself was becoming aware of the all-pervasive nature of his intellectual interests, interests forever inseparable from an intricate conjunction of visual and verbal. The eclecticism of Ruskin's experiences, the complex web of seemingly incompatible juxtapositions, and their tendency to proliferate beyond control, were already present in the early volumes of *Modern Painters*, and the range of inquiry and the kind of wayward interest in new aesthetic juxtapositions that Ruskin demonstrated held a particular resonance for the Pre-Raphaelites. They were attracted to those aforementioned qualities that remain very difficult for readers of Ruskin today, namely the aesthetic, ideological and religious incongruities in his work, together with his dogged persistence with details and issues of seeming artistic inconsequence. More fundamentally they engaged those

14

rich aesthetic possibilities emerging from Ruskin's celebration of the inter-relationship of image and text.

As part of the same condition, the Pre-Raphaelites celebrated Ruskin's reappraisal of the indivisibility of visual perception and representation because it overreached the bounds of artistic convention as taught at the Royal Academy. The Royal Academy teaching received by Millais, Holman Hunt and Rossetti, with its academic preoccupation with drawing from the antique that finally, with graduation to the life class, gave way to an observation of a live body, was very different from Ruskin's absorption in natural objects and his commitment to the study of form in nature. It is not surprising, therefore, that the art students perceived Ruskin's aesthetic theory as a radical alternative. Similar to William Hazlitt's critique of the President of the Royal Academy Joshua Reynolds' theory of ideal form in painting, Ruskin's promotion of embodied vision, of truth to the object perceived, offered aesthetic liberation to the young artists. At the same time, their divergence from received views on contemporary painting ensured to some extent a negative reception for their works. Ruskin's defence emphasized their modernity as characterized fundamentally by their departure from mainstream Victorian artistic practices. Indeed, in the aforementioned 'Letter to *The Times*' 30 May 1851, Ruskin argues that the public's extreme antipathy to the use of colour in Pre-Raphaelite paintings, as expressed by such vituperative critics as Dickens, owes precisely to the fact that 'the only light which we are accustomed to see represented is that which falls on the artist's model in his dim painting-room not that of sunshine in the fields' (*Ruskin* XII, 327). Ruskin's point about the degradation of colour in contemporary painting is one that he had earlier explored in great depth in *Modern Painters I* (especially in the chapter 'Of Truth of Colour'), but it was equally a condition of contemporary British art that, through a commitment to pure pigments and *plein air* painting, the Pre-Raphaelites sought to reform.

If we further consider the Pre-Raphaelites as early readers and mediators of Ruskin at a crucial historical period in which the author was developing, not only an idiosyncratic and highly influential voice, but a particular interdisciplinary method of art-historical analysis drawing upon contemporary debates from

15

the realms of science as well as the arts, we begin to locate poetic and painterly outputs of the group as part of a composite vision, a vision highly self-conscious about the process of its formation. With the Pre-Raphaelites' commitment to a new understanding of visual perception, those complex circumstances of seeing that comprise a modern condition of visuality, and a desire to represent both in language and in paint that which is seen by the embodied human eye, it makes little sense to attempt to isolate Pre-Raphaelite poetry from Pre-Raphaelite visual art. As we shall find, the impetus for the poetry derives from an innovative visual aesthetic and its inextricability from that aesthetic becomes newly meaningful in the light of Ruskin's radically integrated intellectual methods.

It is the case that the famous Pre-Raphaelite dictum, 'go directly to nature, painting what you see', signalling the fantasy of a non-selective eye, indicates at face value a commitment to an unapologetic empiricism. But, as we shall establish, a desire for a radical empirical method collapses into a celebration of its opposite: that which lies beyond optical discovery. Such a movement between the empirical and the transcendental is perhaps most obviously present in Pre-Raphaelite painting and verse in instances of extreme literality, in painting the coming together of a highly representational with a highly symbolic content. Yet, neither Pre-Raphaelite painting nor poetry is interested in a symbolic relationship in which an object represents something other than itself. First and foremost, each element in painting or poem must be readable as itself: the young Christ figure in Millais' *Christ in the House of his Parents*, who bears the stigmata but remains essentially a boy who has injured his hand while helping his carpenter father; the death's head moth in Hunt's *The Hireling Shepherd*, a faithfully observed specimen of natural history which bears its portent visibly on its thorax. If we understand the primacy of the 'literal' symbol in such examples there does not exist a huge difference between the geological detail of the landscape in John Brett's *The Stonebreaker* (1857–8) and that eerily, because entirely naturally, lit one in Ford Madox Brown's *plein air* painting *Pretty Baa Lambs* (1851–9). To be sure, this movement towards the literal symbol, by which the artist seeks to empty the object of any extraneous symbolic value, is a move towards the aestheticism of the later

Rossetti, as influenced by French writers such as Baudelaire and Hugo. Thus, in Rossetti's *The Blue Bower* (1865), in which the figure of a woman sensuously offers herself up to representation, the work of art aspires chiefly to its own materiality. Yet, arguably, the difference between this painting and later 'Aesthetic' canvasses lies chiefly in the fact that in the former the material presence of paint, its intense 'blueness' remains primarily harnessed to recognizable objects rather than more abstract forms. But the profundity of a work such as *The Blue Bower* comes from a movement occurring within the image from form to a type of formlessness; a movement whereby colour is celebrated precisely for transcending its anchorage in an object. It is a similarly striking visual effect, whereby light appears not to be upon objects but within them, that Ruskin pinpoints as most nearly approximated by Turner in a diary entry from Venice 12 May 1841:

> What a delicious afternoon I spent yesterday in St. Mark's – trying to get the local colour of the church [....] Then when I left the square, before the sunset – at it, rather – there was a light such as Turner in his maddest moments never came up to; it turned the masts of the guard frigate into absolute pointed fire, and the woods of the botanic gardens took it in the same way – not as if it were light on them, but in them. (*Diaries* 185–6)

TURNER AND THE PRE-RAPHAELITES

In his pamphlet *Pre-Raphaelitism* of 1851 Ruskin writes:

> I wish it to be understood how every great man paints what he sees or did see, his greatness being indeed little else than his intense sense of fact. And thus Pre-Raphaelitism and Raphaelitism, and Turnerism, are all one and the same, so far as education can influence them. They are different in their choice, different in their faculties, but all the same in this, that Raphael himself, so far as he was great, and all who preceded or followed him who ever were great, became so by painting the truths around them as they appeared to each man's own mind, and not as he had been taught to see them, except by the God who made both him and them. (*Ruskin* XII, 385)

Here, the connection we are exploring between Turner and the

Pre-Raphaelites comes by way of a commitment to Ruskin's well-known phrase 'truth to nature' that endures in the face of teaching, and critical fashion, that finds a different means of expression but retains a foundation in what Ruskin refers to as an 'intense sense of fact'. For Ruskin, as we have found, 'fact' does not simply denote empirically observed or delineated objects but articulates instead embodied vision, in the form of an eye influenced by particular conditions of viewing; an eye open to the nuance of change in a landscape for example, alert to the shifting tones of a bird's plumage or to fluctuating cloud formations. What is more, Ruskin's statement of commensurability recognizes a common link between distinct artistic styles and periods via a stress on painting what the embodied eye sees when, answerable ultimately only to God, it is stripped of convention.

As previously noted, Ruskin's defence of the Pre-Raphaelites, and its connection to his earlier defence of Turner, has at its core a concept of modernity and of what 'modern' paintings might look like. Thus, although in many ways their artistic styles are antithetical, Turner and the Pre-Raphaelites come together conceptually for Ruskin as painters who were radically challenging the status quo. They do so by emphasizing a method of seeing the world emergent in the context of nineteenth century scientific work on the physiology of vision, one that attributed renewed importance to the idiosyncratic eye of an observer. It was an account of vision distinct, for example, from those that relied upon the dominance of mechanical metaphors to articulate processes of seeing. In the recognition of the fluctuating visual capacities of human subjects, notions of empirically observed phenomena become complicated. They do so to the extent that for Ruskin, in such very different styles of painting by Turner and the Pre-Raphaelites, there occur fundamental points of correspondence that in turn blur distinctions between the fundamental philosophical categories of empiricism and transcendentalism. For example, Turner's vast expanses of painted light and water in the extensively entitled *Snow Storm – Steam Boat off a Harbour's Mouth making signals in Shallow Water, and going by the Lead. The author was in the Storm the night the Ariel left Harwich* (1842) and Holman Hunt's faithfully observed harebells in *The Hireling Shepherd* (1851–2) both, in their own ways, frustrate a strict dichotomy between, on the one hand, a relatively abstract and, on the other, a comparatively realist method of representation.[7] What occurs is that, with an equally pressing desire on the part of both painters to explore the physiological circumstances of vision, those seemingly oppositional methods of representation, the abstract and the realist, become less assured such that the philosophical categories of the empirical and the transcendental are newly inflected. Ruskin celebrates the phenomenological aspects of visual perception in Turner's singular method of representing them. Consequently, he called what he regarded one of Turner's 'finest' and misunderstood works, the aforementioned *Snow Storm* 'one of the very grandest statements of sea-motion, mist, and light, that [had] ever been put on canvas, even by Turner' (*Ruskin* III, 571). And it was in fact an attack on this painting together with other works by Turner that prompted Ruskin to begin *Modern Painters*.

Yet, rather predictably, perhaps, curators of the centenary exhibition 'Ruskin, Turner and the Pre-Raphaelites' in 2001, identified Turner's *Snow Storm* as a far cry from Pre-Raphaelite canvases while of course for Ruskin it would not strictly have been so. Indeed, by embracing a subtle conceptual shift Ruskin resolves the apparent paradox of his interest in such different styles as those of Turner and the Pre-Raphaelites. For while Turner most obviously evokes the transcendental by concentrating upon the constituents of visual perception itself, vast expanses of sky and sea for example, the Pre-Raphaelites also do so by rendering naturalistic detail hallucinatory in its visual clarity. To an extent, both painterly methods perplex the eye of the viewer and elicit a response by throwing into relief particular physiological aspects of vision.

Common to Ruskin, Turner and the Pre-Raphaelites, then, is an intention to paint that which an individually embodied eye sees and thereby to represent a faithful transcription of nature. William Holman Hunt's uniquely credible image of Christ in his painting *The Light of the World*, the physical demands he underwent of painting outdoors in moonlight, shares with Turner's artistic methods an impetus to embrace the corporeality of the artist, to regard visual perception as an embodied sense. Both Turner and the Pre-Raphaelites, as Ruskin inter-

19

preted their works, are concerned with painting what the eye sees at particular times, under particular atmospheric conditions. In Holman Hunt's case, as the example of *The Scapegoat* reminds us, such optical fidelity taken to extreme ends could result in curiously unreadable images. The activity of painting an actual goat on the salt-encrusted shores of the Dead Sea, the importance of the presence of the moment, might render the resulting image unintelligible to viewers who did not share the import of the actual experience.[8] Indeed, when Holman Hunt's *Scapegoat* was exhibited, aside from Ruskin's appreciation of exemplary painting of hair and hoof, it was dismissed, likened to the commonplace sheep's head that furnished many a Victorian dinner plate.

'BOTANIZING'

We may witness something of the development of this aesthetic trajectory of 'authenticity', if we consider D. G. Rossetti's well-known poem 'The Woodspurge' from 1856, a poem that Carol Christ drew to our attention in *The Finer Optic*[9] to demonstrate the particular visual imperative of Rossetti's poetry. Contemporary with Ruskin's *Modern Painters III* that Rossetti was reading on its publication, the poem raises questions fundamental to the chapter entitled 'Of the Pathetic Fallacy' from Ruskin's text. Moreover, 'The Woodspurge' also dramatizes those ways in which a condition of Pre-Raphaelite symbolic literality works in poetry as it does in painting. Voicing the impossibility of separating the symbol from its literal incarnation the poem dwells upon the peculiar endurance of natural detail:

> The wind flapped loose, the wind was still,
> Shaken out dead from tree and hill:
> I had walked on at the wind's will, –
> I sat now, for the wind was still.
>
> Between my knees my forehead was, –
> My lips, drawn in, said not Alas!
> My hair was over in the grass,
> My naked ears heard the day pass.
>
> My eyes, wide open, had the run
> Of some ten weeds to fix upon;

Among those few, out of the sun,
The woodspurge flowered, three cups in one.

From perfect grief there need not be
Wisdom or even memory:
One thing then learnt remains to me, –
The woodspurge has a cup of three.

The verse crystallizes the relationship to symbolic representation of a faithful transcription of natural phenomena. The first two lines of the final stanza reject Christian teaching that is compromised, or differently inflected, in the final couplet. To assert that the highly symbolic formation of the flower of the woodspurge, representative of the trinity, exists to be remembered for itself only is also to communicate the inextricability of the established and irrefutable symbolism of the petal formation from the empirically observed flower. Moreover, the final stanza of the poem undermines the authority of symbolism in terms of its ability to represent a 'moral' message: 'from perfect grief there need not be/ Wisdom or even memory'. Thus, a state of 'perfect grief' need not open the subject to an experience of natural phenomena coloured by that state.

The perception of minutiae is liberating for the speaker here because it exists independent of his state of consciousness, reminding him that the perception of nature does not provide primarily a didactic message for the subject. What is more, in its insistence upon a fundamental 'truth', the physical formation of the blossom of the woodspurge, Rossetti's poem echoes Ruskin's account of the gentian in *Modern Painters*, where in his critique of German mysticism Ruskin maintains that the unique blueness of the alpine flower is independent of his perception of it (*Ruskin V*, 202). In Ruskin's claim that the gentian *is* forever blue whether or not he sees it as such, the great 'fact' of blueness overpowers the reasoning capacity. For Ruskin, as for Rossetti's speaker, there is comfort in a conviction that the empirical provides a key to the transcendental but that the former does not exist primarily to serve the latter. For Rossetti's speaker, the simple fact of the configuration of the petals of the woodspurge pitches the literal and the symbolic in an extreme conjunction whereby the literalizing impulse overrides the symbolic in new ways.

Rossetti's painting *Venus Verticordia* (1864–8, cover image) may further demonstrate my point. Influenced by French aestheticism, Rossetti's desire to produce a nude portrait resulted in the half-length figure of Venus represented behind a ledge. The title of the painting 'derives from an invocation to the Roman Goddess of beauty and sensual love to turn the hearts of women to virtue and chastity' but specifically I want to draw attention to the persistence of the exquisite flowers in this painting. I am led to do so by Ruskin. The honeysuckle in the foreground in their various stages of openness, rather than the more uniformly painted roses behind the figure of Venus, frame the image and distance themselves from the painted flesh of the woman very much by their surface difference. In a sense, like Holman Hunt's treatment of the ivy in *The Light of the World*, or in the rendering of the symbolic in literal form in that painting (Christ, metaphorically 'the Light of the World' presented literally holding a lamp), what we have here is a desire to literalize the metaphorical.

Ruskin remarked upon the realism of the honeysuckle in ways resembling those he had used to describe Holman Hunt's painting of the goat in *The Scapegoat*, but for similar reasons he failed to understand either painting. Writing to Rossetti he maintains:

> I purposely used the word 'wonderfully' painted about those flowers. They were wonderful to me, in their realism; awful I can use no other word – in their coarseness; showing enormous power; showing certain conditions of non-sentiment which underlie all you are doing – now – and which make your work, compared to what it used to be – what Fannie's face is to Lizzie's. [10]

To be sure, a conjunction of the conventionally symbolic with the heightened realist elements of the painting frustrates a strict literal/metaphorical dichotomy as explored in 'The Woodspurge'. This tension is very noticeably played out in the proximity to the loosely painted flesh of Venus of the almost crystalline detail of the honeysuckle blossoms. And it is the intense visual shock of these different kinds of painting within the unitary image that Ruskin seeks to fathom in his psychologizing reading.

Rossetti's poem, 'The Honeysuckle' of 1853, adds a further resonance in its play upon symbolic value frustrated. The speaker endures all manner of physical difficulty in order to reach a single stem of wild blossom, but that prize is subsequently undermined when he discovers many honeysuckles growing luxuriantly nearby:

> Thence to a richer growth I came,
> Where, nursed in mellow intercourse,
> The honeysuckles sprang by scores,
> Not harried like my single stem,
> All virgin lamps of scent and dew.

Yet, although faced with the luxury of finer blossoms the speaker casts aside his now paltry bloom, he does so precisely in order *not* to 'pluck' 'any one' of the new superiorly formed flowers. Contrary to its seemingly allegorical form, the poem offers no easy intellectual resolution. Rossetti presents a speaker who recognizes as futile his initial desire, but more fundamentally he figures the honeysuckle as simply all too symbolic and hence in keeping with those flowers that generate Ruskin's extreme reaction to *Venus Verticordia* as cited above. Moreover, Ruskin's concern for what he calls 'conditions of non-sentiment' with which he believes Rossetti to be working in the 1860s is a response to the painting that barely disguises a deep moral antipathy to the painter's involvement with the former prostitute Fanny Cornforth. More significantly, perhaps, Ruskin's simile of 'Fannie's face to Lizzie's' as indicative of a negative shift in Rossetti's painting, belies the extent to which he himself has invested in the figure of Siddal as muse. At one level such investment occurs in both his and Rossetti's individual identifications with the Dante/Beatrice relationship. While Ruskin alludes to Beatrice, Rossetti mythologizes Siddal as a tragic figure whose incarnation as Beatrice cannot be surpassed in paint. Yet, even in such a context of extended metaphorical connection, Ruskin's response to 'conditions of non-sentiment' in *Venus Verticordia* appears to signal more than simply an aversion to finding in his paintings of this period Rossetti's mistress's face occupying the place of the artist's late wife's.

Undoubtedly, in the larger terms of his relationship to the Pre-Raphaelites, Rossetti's predilection for such 'literal' detail as present in the foreground honeysuckle of *Venus Verticordia* confirms Ruskin's specialized attraction to 'botanizing', a botanizing that always entails deep psychological investment.

This is not necessarily a reassuring confirmation, for it brings with it, albeit at an unconscious level, a chain of associations linking back to his fragile mental state. From an early age, to ruminate over what he saw and to attempt to capture it in sketches as well as prose, formed a key part of Ruskin's daily experience. Moreover, he subsequently found in certain Pre-Raphaelite paintings a quality of intense detail that he aspired to achieve in his own drawings. In later life, especially in periods of mental crisis, botanizing, especially over geological specimens, represented for Ruskin a trusted anchor of sanity. At times he dramatically queried this interest, in one instance, fairly late in his life for example, preferring in its place the plumage of birds as a more abstract object of contemplation than even the surface of rocks: 'I have made a great mistake. I have wasted my life with mineralogy, which has led to nothing. Had I devoted myself to birds, their plumage, I might have produced something worth doing.'[11] Nonetheless, the impulse to record visual minutiae remained with Ruskin throughout his life as a form of psychological necessity.

Yet neither was it simply the discipline of concentration, nor the mental rigours of drawing, in which he found comfort during moments of mental turmoil. More generally, he was attracted to the visual force of over-abundance for the access it provided to the transcendental, a more acceptable correlate of the 'non-sentiment' he finds in Rossetti's striking verisimilitude as discussed above. There is, then, a certain irony in those qualities of 'non-sentiment' that Ruskin finds in Rossetti, a process of transference by which he reads in *Venus Verticordia* that very emotional detachment he strives for, but rarely finds, in his own 'botanizing'. Indeed, the use of the simile, 'what Fanny's face is to Lizzie's' discloses the impossibility for Ruskin of a dispassionate response to the painting of flowers given his extreme attachment to Rose La Touche, her wonderfully apposite name, that remains for him forever overtly encoded in a commitment to botanizing.

As we shall find, such an impulse towards a kind of representational excess also provides a key to many of Rossetti's paired works that generate a sense that a single mode of representation is never enough; a visual requires a verbal and a verbal a visual counterpart. In the movement between painted surface of foreground and background, faithfully observed botanical specimens and loosely realized flesh, we find in *Venus Verticordia* an extreme contrast to the more uniformly and insistently empirical methods of Holman Hunt's painting. Indeed, a dark, inscrutable compulsion haunts the work of Rossetti and did so from the first. Yet, Holman Hunt and Rossetti both came under the powerful influence of Ruskin. What is more, such formally antithetical styles as Holman Hunt's and Rossetti's were not anathema to the art critic. Ruskin didn't dismiss Rossetti because initially he possessed less technical facility than either Holman Hunt or Millais, for he accepted that such differences had to be understood as evolving in the intricate conjunction of cultural, technical and psychological concerns played out in the works. Indeed, Ruskin praised Rossetti as a colourist and supported him financially. And while 'empathy' might be too indulgent a term to ascribe to Ruskin's motive for assisting the young artist, without doubt the profoundly psychic imperative that drove Rossetti's art was not lost upon Ruskin. Moreover, an echo of that imperative may be glimpsed in the precarious relationship of Ruskin's life to his own work, in those ways in which his personal preoccupations manifest themselves in his critical responses to Rossetti in what we might describe as involutes. Indeed, they emerge in complex linguistic forms and associations that don't immediately yield up their meanings. In fact, as we shall shortly find, the two men became psychically as well as artistically involved; the entangled relationship of life to art that dogged the Pre-Raphaelites more generally, especially Rossetti, was played out in the preoccupations and repetitions of Ruskin's work.

1

One tiny calf-bound volume

Accounts of the Pre-Raphaelites usually begin in London in 1848 with the circumstances of the group's formation by those art students at the Royal Academy. But I want to begin now twenty-one years subsequent to that, on the evening of 5 October 1869. That night a small group of men gathered in Highgate Cemetery in north London to exhume the body of Elizabeth Eleanor Siddal the wife of the painter, poet and foremost Pre-Raphaelite Dante Gabriel Rossetti. The purpose of the disinterment was to retrieve a manuscript book of D. G. Rossetti's poems that he had buried with his wife in a gesture of self-sacrifice following her death in 1862. The proposed collection had been advertised for publication as *Dante at Verona and Other Poems* at the end of 1861. Charles Augustus Howell, a notorious 'dealer' and former secretary of Ruskin, H. V. Tebbs, a lawyer friend of the poet (whose role was to witness items taken from the grave), and Dr Llewellyn Williams 'engaged by Howell to disinfect the manuscript', comprised the macabre vignette that was to impact considerably upon Rossetti's poetic reputation. The team, whose work was lit by lantern and a fire burning at the edge of the grave, so the story goes, had little trouble accessing the contents of the coffin that, according to Rossetti's later account, were in 'perfect' condition. This was not the case, however, with the book of poems itself. William Michael Rossetti tells us, for example, that the pages of the poem 'Jenny' 'had a great worm-hole right through' them 'so that only the ends of the lines were intact' (DW 886). And, writing shortly afterwards to his friend the painter Ford Madox Brown, D. G. Rossetti declared 'a sad wreck' what he simply termed 'those papers'(DW 886).

It is certain that Rossetti deliberated before performing this reversal of his gesture of self-sacrifice, of manifesting his second thoughts about the poems. As Marsh reminds us, 'exhumation was strictly regulated to prevent grave-robbing' and permission had to be sought from the Secretary of State 'with the grave-owner's knowledge and consent' (Marsh 377). The fact that Rossetti's mother owned the grave, and he didn't want to disclose his intentions to her, posed a problem for him that he was able to sidestep, because the new Home Secretary, 'his old friend Henry Bruce departed from strict rules for [him]' (Marsh 374). Biographical evidence points to the fact that Rossetti was forever disturbed by the event, and towards the end of his life he suffered fits of 'delusion' which appear to have represented a deep regret at having opened 'Lizzie's' grave and a strong sense of 'self-blame regarding her death' (Marsh 374). That death remains somewhat unresolved. The cause, an overdose of laudanum, the popular nineteenth century form of taking opium dissolved in brandy, was clear enough to her husband and to the doctors who attended Siddal in 1862. But the alleged presence of a note discovered by Rossetti and disclosed only to his friend and fellow artist Ford Madox Brown, who is said to have burnt it, compromised a notion of accidental death. Consequently, the poet would internalize his wife's suicide. Hence the burial of the manuscript as an act of self-punishment, and recognition of his responsibility for her fate.

I fast forward to this graveyard scene, the stuff of sensation fiction of the same period, in part to acknowledge the degree of sensationalism that has defined Rossetti's reputation and by association that of the Pre-Raphaelite group more generally, but also to foreground the problematic image/text relation. In this study, the burial and disinterment of the poems will stand as an unorthodox reminder not only of the sensationalist legacy that one must negotiate as a reader of the Pre-Raphaelites but also of how, most fundamentally by an extreme act of resurrection, 'words' become 'things'. As members of a self-declared brotherhood the Pre-Raphaelites bore the dubious privilege of being courted and simultaneously undermined by the nature of their celebrity. Some would say that Rossetti was self-styled in this regard, that his extravagant life-style, his penchant for wombats, armadillos and former prostitutes was none other than bohemian attention seeking. In such a narrative he is chiefly remembered for those poems that went to the grave and back, for his garden menagerie in Cheyne Walk, Chelsea and for his paintings of 'fleshly' women. Thereby, he is not so well remembered for his poetry, or for his contribution to an innovative visual and verbal aesthetic that extended conceptually way beyond its initial Pre-Raphaelite remit of 1848. Rather in the manner of the rumours that accrued to the cause of Ruskin's annulled marriage to Effie Gray, the relationship to Rossetti's career of the exhumation has been rendered out of all proportion.[1] Or has it? The very fact that readers have felt inclined to return to the disinterment discloses particular anxieties, desires and fantasies not only engendered by the event itself but also by its recall. Moreover, as we shall find, fascination for the exhumation is not entirely separable from those complex physical and psychological states articulated by the retrieved poems themselves, conditions that characterized in larger terms the preoccupations of Pre-Raphaelitism. Rather than dismissing the odd extra-textual life of Rossetti's poems, therefore, we should instead examine those ways in which it might provide a fitting context from which to begin to rethink the Pre-Raphaelite movement as a whole.

In part, the fascination of the tale for readers of Victorian culture is simply a response to the macabre but nonetheless miraculous resurrection of that which was lost to the world: a seemingly irreversible gesture reversed. However, for those actually and emotionally involved in the retrieval of the notebook, there must also have emerged a strangely heightened sense of the material presence of the grey calf-bound volume itself, of those poems Rossetti had so wanted to revisit. To be certain, in the process of its retrieval the manuscript becomes something other than a potential book of poetry; re-figured is the status of the book as a material object. Indeed, its extreme condition, its bitter smell and the fact that it was 'soaked through and through' (Marsh 377) meant that once regained Rossetti's notebook could no longer simply be words on a page becoming, instead, a thing closer to the corporeal. As a synecdoche for the very mutability of the body owing to its sustained proximity to the decaying corpse of Siddal, the manuscript must bear the mark of death thereafter. Moreover, in a profound irony, the event at Highgate Cemetery throws into troubled relief Rossetti's desire for immortality through his

28

verse, a motive he would forever strenuously deny as a reason for his actions.

As Jan Marsh informs us, Rossetti 'had his first sight of the manuscript [two weeks later] at Dr Williams' house. Still wet, it had a dreadful smell, from decay and disinfectants' (Marsh 377). Such factors could only have obscured the purpose for which Rossetti sought to consult the book, namely to restore those poems – 'A Last Confession', 'Dante at Verona', 'The Bride's Chamber' and 'Jenny' – of which he had no fair copy. In a further sense, the odour of its pages, a terrible mixture of decay and sanitation, became both a constant reminder of the impossibility of erasing the book's extreme history and also a sign of Rossetti's guilt compounded, guilt, that is, pertaining to the circumstances of his wife's death and associated with his inability finally to let his poems 'die' with her. Instead of encountering the restored poems as a poet alive to words and sounds Rossetti first reaches them via his olfactory sense, by the pungency of those chemicals used to mask the smell of decay. Yet while the book of poems would remain thus locked in an aesthetic of death, its more immediate fate was to be published in 1870, together with poems that would in 1881 go to make up the sonnet sequence, doomed from the start by Rossetti's enduring fear of bad reviews and unfittingly entitled *Towards The House of Life*.[2]

The incident of the manuscript book of poems rescued from the grave brings to the fore a particular relationship between verbal and visual, whereby the primary visibility of words (as linguistic marks) substitutes for their signification. Simultaneously, as we shall find, there occurs in the process a compromised distinction between the visual arts and the verbal or linguistic ones that is at the core of the aesthetic of Pre-Raphaelitism. For Rossetti, the obliteration by time, so to speak, of parts of the poem 'Jenny' means that the inky forms of words themselves approximate pictures as they hover, in the reader's visual field, at relative points of intelligibility. Such an altered visual experience, a heightened hallucinatory quality as induced by the marred book, stresses the sense of sight as determined by psychological factors, a type of the Ruskinian grotesque in which imagination fills in conceptual gaps. It is a quality that Rossetti had earlier alluded to in a letter of 1845 in which, witnessing a scene from cliff-tops at Hastings, he dwells upon the psychological aspect of the creative process; a quality to which Ruskin had also drawn attention in defining Rossetti's work as 'a true unison of the grotesque with realistic power'.[3]

By extension, and subsequent to Rossetti's action of retrieving the poems, we may identify possibilities for revising an implied split between painting and poetry that continued to intrigue Rossetti throughout his life. Not only that, but the exhumation puts a very different slant on a Biblical notion of the word made flesh. For, words as manifest in the small calf-bound book with its damaged leaves come to stand for the body of the beloved that may be neither resurrected nor adequately represented. In a simple act of imaginative displacement the book becomes the ruined body and those verses 'robbed' from the grave a residue of its antithesis.

To some extent then so compelling were its details that we as readers may be forgiven for our investment in the exhumation. Without a doubt Rossetti was haunted for the rest of his life by having disturbed the grave and repeatedly felt impelled to justify his actions. In a letter to his friend and fellow poet Swinburne explaining the retrieval of the manuscript Rossetti writes that 'art was the only thing for which she [Siddal] felt very seriously. Had it been possible to her, I should have found the book on my pillow the night she was buried; and could she have opened the grave no other hand would have been needed' (DW 892). The claim that Elizabeth Siddal would have renounced immediately her husband's gesture of self-sacrifice in order to prioritize the higher realm of art provides an imagined scenario in which her placing the poems upon Rossetti's pillow eroticizes the volume and complicates the fantasized gesture. Two issues thereby merge in Rossetti's retrospective wishful thinking that make it difficult finally to extricate a notion of literary worthiness from its supernatural context. Firstly, Rossetti appeared convinced that his wife had communicated with him from the grave to the extent that she wished him to take back the poems. Yet, secondly and ironically, the manifest forms of her communication undermine a sense that Siddal's literary and artistic conviction simply would have been sufficient in itself to justify the act of exhumation. Rossetti posits Siddal's aesthetic commitments as adequate reason for action but compromises his reasoning by relegating her agency to a supernatural sphere: what he regards as the sign of a chaffinch. Certainly as far as his friends such as Swinburne were concerned Rossetti's belief in his wife's artistic convictions, together with her own artistic and poetic output, would have been sufficient to justify the disinterment. At the same time, Rossetti was clearly convinced of the fact that his secrecy on the matter of the poems would not endure indefinitely, that invariably 'the truth must ooze out'. Additionally, there is a pervasive sense in which there had endured among Rossetti's close friends an unspoken agreement that the fabled book of verse would be returned to them. Swinburne expresses in his response a long-repressed desire that 'none could have given [him] a truer or deeper pleasure'. He writes, 'to our nearest friends I would never allow myself to talk on the subject; but none the less I have thought often and bitterly of the loss sustained' (Marsh 376). And William Michael Rossetti registers less than surprise at his brother's disclosure of having got back the poems.

Odd, perhaps, these investments but let's ponder further the transformation of this little book, its heightened materiality, as a means by which to approach in wider terms the highly self-conscious and problematical relationship of language to image, of poetry to painting in Pre-Raphaelitism. To begin with, one might conjecture that the book becomes for Rossetti not simply a form of the beloved's body but a complex substitute for his own. While upon his beloved's death the poet does not ape the gesture of Shakespeare's Hamlet throwing himself into Ophelia's grave, he instead offers up his words as flesh. Having done so, however, he must eventually take back the offering, stealthily revoke that action designed to approximate his burial alive alongside the beloved. But if, following this line of reasoning, the poems substitute for the poet's body, what are the implications of restoring them to the world? If, in the transcription of decayed words something of the new materiality of the language of those poems is eluded, there remains a kind of residue at the figurative level corresponding with the retrieved and subsequently discarded book, how might we begin to articulate this hesitant or newly determined relationship between original and copy?

Several commentators have pointed out the relative oddity of Rossetti's desire to retrieve the poems since he had versions of each of them in one form or another. By this reckoning, it would seem as if for the poet a drive to retrieve the book became in itself all-consuming, tantalizing in part for the shame and self-disgust that drive aroused in him, perhaps because the poems had taken a kind of imprint of the corporeal which he had wanted their language to convey. Rather, in the act of retrieval the apparent gap between words and the sensuous physicality of things had been closed such that the eternal nature of language had become little more than the mutability of the body. What is certain is that Rossetti tried to hide the possible association of his act with a desire for poetic fame. In so doing, though, he produced a narrative for literary history that bears at its centre an exhumation that has made little sense for readers in terms other than those of poetic fame. In truth, Rossetti's preoccupation with having disturbed the grave represents more than shame at what others might perceive as a blatant desire for literary recognition. It represents a sense of his having violated a boundary, of having penetrated what should have remained sealed.

Most essentially, never again after 1869 could this manuscript book be simply a book of poems. Not only does the volume come to stand in for the body as I've suggested, but in larger terms it creates a merger of the material with the immaterial, of the empirical with the transcendental, of language and vision, in a manner characteristic of Pre-Raphaelitism as a whole. There is not a little irony in the additional fact that the extreme act of digging up poems obscures an equally extreme project of Pre-Raphaelitism to radically interrogate that enigmatic relationship between visible and invisible as uniquely expressed in the sister arts analogy (the relationship of painting to poem). More specifically, the retrieved manuscript as words defaced by time and death haunts Rossetti, for while he may transcribe the lost poems, something of what they have become entirely eludes reproduction. This approximate quality captured in the meta-morphosis of the book comes close to articulating the aesthetic of Pre-Raphaelitism as residing in a new relationship of language to image, of poetry to painting.

The fact that we too as twenty-first century readers find it difficult to accept the retrieval of the poems as an act divorced from Rossetti's desire for renown provides a key to what has been a larger fate of Pre-Raphaelitism. The investment of the

Pre-Raphaelites in the corporeal has been at the same time played down and overexposed. For certain, it is to a large extent in the poets' and painters' attitudes to the body, the relationship of corporeality to spirituality, that their particular aesthetic finds its purpose. For the Pre-Raphaelites, artistic and poetic preoccupation with the body was captured in the sister arts analogy and in a discourse of ekphrasis that focused a relation between the visual and linguistic arts. Thus, as the rather extreme case of Rossetti here demonstrates, in order to understand that Pre-Raphaelite aesthetic we must rethink fundamentally a concept of bodily indeterminacy as expressed in a type of ekphrastic relationship.

Ekphrasis itself is a rather indeterminate classical aesthetic category. While it may straightforwardly describe in a text a visual image – a verbal conjuring of an artefact since lost – equally ekphrasis may refer to an invented image.[4] Moreover, for the Pre-Raphaelites the subtle balancing of visual and verbal in the ekphrastic relation is perhaps located most intriguingly in the poetic figure of the hermaphrodite in which the dissolving of sexual difference also articulates that very difference subtended between visual and verbal modes. As we shall find in Chapter 5, Swinburne's figure of the hermaphrodite upon which questions of obscenity become focused represents most overtly such a willingness to court indeterminacy or, more precisely, to figure forth the relation of words to things that Rossetti's decayed words embody.

The haunting condition of Rossetti's calf-bound volume will call us back periodically. But for now, as readers, we come to the poems with retrospective knowledge of the exhumation in all its complexity. However, for the painters and poets involved there obtained a curious prospective aspect to this episode. Afterall, Millais had painted Elizabeth Siddal in the early 1850s as the drowning figure of Ophelia, the human fate already anticipated long before in the literary context. Let's now consider further the figure of the dead woman that not only haunts this well-known episode from literary history but also resonates throughout the aesthetic of Pre-Raphaelitism more generally. But let us not fail to remember, in the process, a painting of one particular dead man, in whose suicide poetic production was deeply implicated.

2

Several dead women and one dead man

John Everett Millais rowed back and forth across the Hogsmill River at Ewell to paint the densely planted bank for his work *Ophelia* (1851–2) (Plate 1) showing the tragic character from Shakespeare's *Hamlet* at the point of her death by drowning.[1] While figures of dead women are common currency in nineteenth century literature and painting the Pre-Raphaelites take up the motif in singular ways. They also broach the subject of dead men in paintings such as Hunt's *Rienzi* and most spectacularly in Henry Wallis' equally striking *The Death of Chatterton* (1855–6) (Plate 2).[2] Though Millais' *Ophelia*, first exhibited at the Royal Academy in 1852, has become an uncontested emblem of Pre-Raphaelitism, in curious ways Wallis' *The Death of Chatterton* amounts to its haunting double. Wallis depicts the young beautiful late-eighteenth century poet Thomas Chatterton lying dead in a poor garret room, having taken his own life with arsenic. When the seventeen year-old's claim to have discovered works by 'Rowley', a medieval priest, was discredited – Chatterton himself had invented them – he committed suicide penniless in the East End of London. In Wallis' painting the torn up pieces of manuscript spilling from the trunk, signalling his act of 'forgery', occupy the bottom left of the composition while a phial emptied of its poison lies near his open hand. Ruskin wrote of it: 'faultless and wonderful: a most noble example of the great school. Examine every inch: it is one of the pictures which intend and accomplish the entire placing before your eyes of an actual fact – and that a solemn one. Give it much time' (*Ruskin* XIV, 60). But that 'solemn' and 'actual fact' to which Ruskin here refers is not at all clear. Is it the

1 John Everett Millais, *Ophelia* (1851–2) Tate Britain

fact of suicide? The forgerer made tragic and effeminate in death: the 'fact' of bodily indeterminacy as standing in for aesthetic indeterminacy?

Without doubt, *The Death of Chatterton* raises the issue of effeminacy prior to D. G. Rossetti's and Swinburne's poetry. Indeed, the androgyny of the beautiful 'boy' perhaps goes some way to explaining why, when exhibited at the Manchester Art Treasures Exhibition in 1857, the painting famously required two policemen to protect it from an admiring crowd. The pallor of Chatterton's face, his striking shock of auburn hair, recalls that of the earlier 'Ophelia', exemplar of the school of Pre-Raphaelitism. In addition, mythologized most famously by Keats and Wordsworth, Chatterton represents an approximate double for Rossetti's later image of himself as tragic poet. Towards the end of his life Rossetti became fascinated by the fate of Chatterton when his friend Theodore Watts-Dunton was editing selections of the poet's works for the third volume of T. H. Ward's *English Poets*.[3] Moreover, in his sonnet of 1880 Rossetti dwells in particular upon 'the grave unknown' and the 'unrecorded face' of Chatterton.[4]

By twists of fate, both Wallis' and Millais' paintings subsequently became iconic owing both to the painters' rare technical virtuosity, and also to the biographical intrigue of the models. The wife of the poet George Meredith, who modelled for Wallis, would two years later elope with the artist while, just over a decade after Millais painted Elizabeth Siddal as 'Ophelia', she would die of an overdose of laudanum. In *Ophelia* the hallucinatory realism of the image – the verisimilitude of animated hands beckoning from the water in a gesture of surrender – arrests the ambivalence of the states of death and ecstasy. Moreover, it is a formally complex image, claustrophobic in its faithful rendering of intense green foliage that occupies the entire picture-plane offering no relief of sky. The doomed Ophelia is painted in such a way that, as Geoffrey Hemstedt has written, 'landscape has become a bowering enclosure of greenery, an effect emphasized by the curving top of the frame'[5]. And Millais painstakingly rendered that enclosure in part because the invention of photography had also made more urgent for artists the phenomenon of presence. That is to say, he rowed back and forth across the river to paint its bank because it was

2 Henry Wallis, *The Death of Chatterton* (1855–6) Tate Britain

now possible to depict, by way of photography, what he saw there and desired to represent. Millais did so, though, not in an attempt to compete with a photograph but rather because the possibility of photographic representation re-defined a concept of what it might mean for an artist to be present at the occasion of perception and, concomitantly, representation. A concept of having been present became a new aesthetic necessity that would play itself out most unabashedly in the *plein air* painting of the Impressionists. For, a photograph's revolutionary ability to capture by physical and chemical actions presence at a locale makes newly imperative (as in the example of Millais) the painter's relationship to the physicality of the object and to a sense of place. In the case of Wallis' *Chatterton* such a photographic imperative resonates most strikingly in James Robinson's stereo-slide of 1860, a photographic recreation of the scene of Wallis' painting. More specifically, that particular photograph deemed to have infringed copyright law raised fundamental questions about the status in relation to painting of the relatively new medium of photography.[6]

Owing to its biographical connections, Millais' *Ophelia* significantly affects the narrative we have so far been tracing. Elizabeth Siddal modelled for the drowning figure and, as the popular story goes, caught cold while posing for long periods in a bath of water warmed by candles. Moreover, in a further impending congruence between art and life the 'mad' and suicidal Ophelia is here 'played' by an artist's model who will go on to kill herself. Thus, a tendency towards pre-figurative symbolism so favoured by the Pre-Raphaelites in equally early canvases as Millais' *Christ in the House of his Parents* (1849–50) and Holman Hunt's *The Hierling Shepherd* (1851–2), later to become in Oscar Wilde's celebrated maxim a condition of life mimicking art, will be found to have been at work here, too, in *Ophelia*. What is more, we may retrospectively attribute to Ruskin a nominal presence at the exhumation of Siddal's body. Suffice it to say, he haunts Millais' *Ophelia* such that it becomes difficult to extricate from his own life a tragic staging of the death of Shakespeare's heroine, and more generally of the beautiful young woman. In the manner of Siddal as 'Ophelia' the differently doomed Ruskin is to be found embowered in a now famous portrait also painted by Millais. Ruskin commissioned Millais to paint his portrait at Brig O'Turk at the mouth of Glenfinlas in Scotland, writing to his father 6 July 1853: 'We shall have the two most wonderful torrents in the world, Turner's St Gothard and Millais' Glenfinlas'.[7] What is more, circumstances surrounding the subsequent production of the painting *John Ruskin* during 1853–4 are as sensational as those pertaining to *Ophelia* and indeed *Chatterton*. For Millais produced it during his stay in Scotland with Ruskin and his wife Effie Gray, a trip that would lead to the annulment of Ruskin's marriage in 1854 and cast a slur over his hope of future fulfilment in love.

Like 'Ophelia', Ruskin appears in the portrait enshrined in the geologically rich landscape that he so loved to record. Not only does the format of the canvas share the arched top of Millais' earlier painting but also the composition is similarly condensed such that water, rock and lichens fill the whole without that recessional outlet normally provided by sky. But there exists a further biographical association. The disempowered Ruskin, condemned to ridicule for his reputed lack of sexual potency, had supported Siddal's creative work financially. As her patron granting an annual stipend of one hundred and fifty pounds in return for first refusal on her paintings and drawings Ruskin had ensured Siddal a valuable amount of financial independence. Additionally, in recognition of Millais' prodigious talent, he served as mentor to the young artist. Curiously, following the annulment of his marriage Ruskin continued to write about Millais as though nothing had happened. His father, however, refused to allow Millais' portrait of his son to be exhibited; it was shown finally for the first time at the Fine Art Society in 1884. Yet, not only did the portrait evolve as the marriage dissolved, but the distress caused to Ruskin by the saga of the annulment and the charges of impotence that he faced would not find their fullest expression until years later in his thwarted love for Rose La Touche (who herself became insane) and in those repeated bouts of his madness that accompanied his hopeless love for her.[8] Retrospectively, then, Millais' 'Glenfinlas' portrait holds the key to unspeakable sadness and trauma for Ruskin, as does his *Ophelia* for Rossetti.

Between the visual and verbal forms of Ruskin's work there

exists an involute of the relation to Millais' *Ophelia* and his *John Ruskin* of the disturbed mental states of Rossetti and Ruskin. For the paintings operate as vehicles of prophecy: the future encoded in their details if only we might know where to find it. In the first, Millais' *Ophelia*, a condition of futurity marks the blatant symmetry of suicide for suicide, while in the second, Millais' *Ruskin*, it endures in the stifling atmosphere and quality of restraint that the painting captures formally. It might not surprise us to further learn that this quality of prophecy was one of the most profound conceptual potentialities of the new and contemporaneous invention of photography, one to which the early twentieth century critic Walter Benjamin was especially drawn. Those early photographs of the 1840s prior to the rapid commercialization of the medium for Benjamin convey most magically such a quality of temporal disruption.[9] They harbour the potential to suggest the future in the present moment captured (subsequently past) in the 'snapshot' of the image.

Such a quality of prophecy is analogously present in Pre-Raphaelite canvases that lend a hallucinatory quality to their intense realist mode, a quality of seeing beyond empirical detail or, in the case of Wallis' *Chatterton*, a 'solemn actual fact'. It is a quality of 'space' that photography captures that is equally a quality of 'time', a photographic condition that Elizabeth Barrett refers to as one of singular 'nearness'.[10] In recalling the material circumstances of the annulment of Ruskin's marriage to Effie Gray, Millais' 'Glenfinlas' portrait conjures by association his subsequent attachment to Rose La Touche that long-exceeded her premature death in 1875. As with other Pre-Raphaelite canvases, the painting also manifests those elaborate ways in which Ruskin's extreme emotional attachment again encodes itself in a sustained commitment to 'botanizing'.

In 1875 Ruskin produced a pencil sketch of Rose, known as 'Rose La Touche on her deathbed'.[11] It is not literally a deathbed sketch. Her disapproving parents would not have allowed him that privilege but in essence it serves as one; she died on 25 May of that year and Ruskin had last seen her three months before on 25 February. The woman in her twenties is propped upright in bed with wild hair and startled expression: wide eyes look beyond the artist/viewer. There is an incredible intimacy about this sketch of La Touche in her sickness that requires us to question our focus upon sexual intimacy over other kinds of intimacy in Ruskin's life. Owing to the dissimilarity of the sketch to Ruskin's other portraits of his beloved Rose critics question the provenance of the drawing whose existence only became known to J. H. Whitehouse in 1937. However, the private moment captured is not incompatible with the painful intimacy revealed in other sketches by Ruskin, nor in the following account given by him to the artist Francesca Alexander of his last meeting with La Touche:

> Of course she was out of her mind in the end; one evening in London she was raving violently till far into the night; they could not quiet her. At last they let me into her room. She was sitting up in bed; I got her to lie back on the pillow, and lay her head in my arms as I knelt beside it. They left us, and she asked me if she should say a hymn, and she said, 'Jesus, lover of my soul' to the end, and then fell back tired and went to sleep. And I left her.[12]

In this brief record the reader is struck not only by the force of devotion shown by Ruskin but also by his continuing disempowerment: no longer at the mercy of his own parents' decisions but of Rose's parents who control his admittance to her sick room. But in this account and others that disclose Ruskin's complex desire for the woman whom he had loved since she was a child we find a very different portrait than that generally circulated of a man exempt from intimate relationships with women. Ruskin's tragic relationship to La Touche, never consummated, never emotionally resolved, throws light back upon the annulled marriage to Gray, and to a letter which as Helena Michie points out, re-frames the annulment, for reasons of non-consummation (Mitchie 8). In this letter Ruskin refers to a repetition of acts performed on that fateful wedding night in a way that complicates our understanding of the apparently well-rehearsed event. Writing to Effie in 1849, having made the very journey with his parents which they had planned for their honeymoon over a year before but that had been prevented by revolutions in Europe, and still promising her that the marriage would someday be consummated, Ruskin says:

> I expect a line from my dearest love tomorrow at Sens; Do you know, pet, it seems almost a dream to me that we have been married: I look

forward to meeting you; and to your *next* bridal night; and to the time when I shall again draw your dress from your snowy shoulders: and lean my cheek upon them, as if you were still my betrothed only; and I had never held you in my arms.[13]

Most curious about this letter, given the subsequent events of the annulment, is the anticipated pleasure of repetition: 'when I shall *again* draw the dress from your snowy shoulders'. It is odd that Ruskin alludes to the 'next' bridal night, juxtaposing it with the first as 'almost a dream', as if entirely natural for there to be more than one. But the final line that distinguishes 'betrothed' from 'bride', a fantasy of return to a pre-married state is complex in a legal and Biblical context in which Ruskin has 'yet' to *know* Effie as a wife. If, as it seems, he envisages a fantasy of *pre*-nuptial bliss his words beg the question of what in the absence of sexual relations the nuptials have provided that make him want to revisit a time prior to them. His comment is intriguing not least for the way in which it complicates an understanding of the circumstances of the annulment and focuses psychological complexities of his life and work that dovetail with those of D. G. Rossetti. But, it also prompts us to consider those ways in which for Ruskin desire tends to figure intervolved linguistic and pictorial structures of loss.

Both actual and fictional figures of women lost to death haunted Ruskin and Rossetti throughout their lives, manifesting themselves in intricate symbolic literary and art historical references. For Ruskin, following the death of Rose la Touche the figure of Carpaccio's 'St Ursula'[14] assumed a particularly compelling resonance while for Rossetti, as we shall find, following the loss of Siddal, Dante's Beatrice and the sub-terranean figure of Proserpine figured repeatedly in his work. It was the nineteenth-century American writer Edgar Allan Poe who famously remarked that 'the death of a beautiful woman is unquestionably, the most poetical topic in the world', and Elizabeth Bronfen in *Over her Dead Body* has taken up Poe's dictum to explore the figure of the ubiquitous image of the dead woman in a range of historical periods and contexts. Elizabeth Siddal provides a case study for Bronfen, as a woman who lived the life of 'the volatile, etherealized creature of purity and taintedness she was figured as in the artist's rendition' (Bronfen 171). Moreover, Bronfen explores the conjunction of art, death and femininity in a range of western historical contexts to find that viewers enjoy 'representations of death in art' specifically 'because they occur in a realm clearly delineated as not life, or not real, even as they refer to the basic fact of life we know but choose not to acknowledge too overtly' (Bronfen x). The formula she describes, 'death by proxy', resembles the vicarious pleasure of the Burkean sublime whereby 'sublimity' is inherent in terror 'staged' rather than in the actual experience of that condition. According to Bronfen, however, it is the 'feminine body' in particular that is key to such delight in death. Since it operates as 'a superlative site of alterity, culture uses art to dream the deaths of beautiful women'. In such a scheme, linguistic, and visual representations of dead 'feminine' bodies enable culture to 'repress and articulate its unconscious knowledge of death which it fails to foreclose even as it cannot express it directly' (Bronfen x).

From the first, as the case of 'Ophelia' testifies, Pre-Raphaelite painters articulated figures of dead women. But Pre-Raphaelite poets did so too especially in their short-lived periodical *The Germ* that embodies a radical desire to haunt the spaces between established visual and verbal disciplines. Yet curiously, perhaps in a consolidation of their own distance from those representations of dead women, the Pre-Raphaelites confound in various ways the notion of a passive female muse upon whose perfect stilled body viewers may experience the vicarious pleasure of death staged: the plenitude of a body in death. As stated, for Rossetti the iconic figure of Beatrice provided an enduring model with which Ruskin shared a profound connection via his complex relationship with the tragic figure of Rose La Touche. For both men, the figure of Beatrice was prophetic of an unspeakable connection to a dead beloved. But Beatrice also focused the painting/poetry relation through the figure of Dante as poet arrestingly depicted by Rossetti in the act of '*drawing* an angel on the anniversary of the first death of Beatrice'. In that sense the iconic figure of Beatrice marks out a pathway deviating somewhat from the one Bronfen highlights. The same is true of Christina Rossetti's conjuring of 'dead' poetic 'I's. As we shall find, rather than identifiably female 'dead' subjects, there emerge in the twinned visual and verbal aesthetic of Pre-Raphaelitism more indeterminate ones. In Swinburne's and

43

Simeon Solomon's work these coalesce conspicuously in the hermaphroditic body. Indeed, the figure of the hermaphrodite appears as most able to realize (either in plastic or linguistic terms) the uniquely porous or 'doubled' relationship between Pre-Raphaelite poem and picture, word and image.

3

Ut Pictura Poesis: early Pre-Raphaelite Poetry and the case of *The Germ*

From the first, figures of dead women appeared not only in Pre-Raphaelite painting but also in poetry as evidenced by works published in the short-lived periodical *The Germ* which ran for four issues in 1850.[1] *The Germ* is key to an understanding of both writers and painters since it allows us to find, in an embryonic stage of development, the particular twinning of the visual and the verbal central to the early rationale of the Pre-Raphaelites. As the contents of the journal testify, poetry and both fictional and non-fictional prose were central to the aims of the group. However, *The Germ* was a commercial failure; folding after a run of four months, each of the single editions never sold more than two hundred copies. The journal has been regarded as a somewhat contradictory product of Pre-Raphaelitism owing to a disjunction between its physical appearance – its heavy Gothic typeface – and its claims to a radical stance on religion and morality in art. Yet, the significance of the sub-title, 'Thoughts Towards Nature and Art' that came to replace the original title in the February issue and encodes a vital reference to Ruskin, provides recognizable grounds for the twinned mediums of word and visual image that it would continue to promote. Moreover, as I've argued elsewhere, the replacement title advertised the very intertextual nature of the journal, thereby intervening in the rigid genre division and 'sister arts analogies of reviewers' (Smith 123).

Dante Gabriel Rossetti's 'My Sister's Sleep' appeared in the first issue of the magazine. W. M. Rossetti believes it to be dated before his brother's 'The Blessed Damozel' and 'therefore before

May 1847' (*Germ* 8). Remarking upon Dante Gabriel's early use of what was to become known as the '*In Memoriam* rhyme-scheme' following the publication of Tennyson's poem of that name in 1850, he goes on to make much of his brother's later 'distaste' for the poem, maintaining that D. G. Rossetti 'only reluctantly reprinted it in his *Poems* 1870. At the same time, W. M. Rossetti makes the rather odd claim that 'this poem was written long before the Pre-Raphaelite movement began' while adding that it 'none the less [...] shows in an eminent degree one of the influences which guided that movement; the intimate intertexture of a spiritual sense with a material form; small actualities made vocal of lofty meanings' (*Germ* 8). In fact the poem could not have been written 'long before' the movement began (at most a year or so) but W. M. Rossetti's comment upon the poem's 'intimate intertexture of a spiritual sense with a material form' interestingly recognizes his brother's drive to manifest the transcendental in the empirically observed, such that the minute might serve as a key to the infinite.

'My Sister's Sleep' exemplifies the ailing figure of a woman central to a Pre-Raphaelite aesthetic. Here, as in Christina Rossetti's poem 'After Death', we find a vividly evoked death chamber marked by the silence and loyal watchfulness of its inhabitants. But unlike his sister's emphasis upon the perspective of the dead woman and her imaginative construction of an other from the position of a dead subject, D. G. Rossetti here creates a poetic 'I' that frames the plight of the mother. The poem is clearly also about the speaker's own grief as mediated through that of a mother on losing her daughter at the emotive time of Christmas Eve. By way of complex sequence and chronology, the verse subtly distinguishes between the states of sleep and death as freshly realized ones. The reader is affected not so much by the speaker's sister's death as by the shock expressed in the poem at the obfuscation by sleep of death: 'She stooped an instant, calm and tired;/But suddenly turned back again/And all her features seemed in pain/With woe, and her eyes gazed and yearned'.

In a contemporary Victorian context, the image of a young woman on her deathbed was one that also came to preoccupy artists and photographers. In addition to the figure of Ophelia already considered we find examples such as 'Fading Away'

1858 by the popular Victorian photographer Henry Peach Robinson (1830–1901) depicting 'a young consumptive surrounded by her family in her final moments'.[2] Contemporary objection to Robinson's photograph centred on the fact that the image manufactured a private moment of impending grief; a subject for which the 'unique' realism of the medium was inappropriate. The composite (printed from five negatives on to a single sheet of paper) surmounts a technical 'impossibility' – that of photographing such a group of figures indoors in a single exposure. But critics precisely objected to Robinson's tampering with the medium since it violated one of the key principles of photographic 'truth': its record of a specific temporal moment. At the same time, contemporary viewers deemed the subject matter indelicate; Robinson had invaded the death chamber at the most private of moments: '"Fading Away" is a subject which I do not like, and I wonder Mr Robinson should have allowed his fancy to fix on it; it is a picture no one could hang up in a room, and revert to with pleasure' (Smith 84). Vehement critical reaction to Robinson's photograph raises not only ethical issues of the photographically imaged 'death' as a subject for popular consumption but also allows us to newly situate Christina Rossetti's poetic interest in such scenarios.

Christina Rossetti is rarely read in terms of a Pre-Raphaelite aesthetic. While clearly by dint of her gender she was excluded from the concept of a brotherhood she was heavily involved in the early stages of the movement, modelling for several paintings and contributing seven poems to *The Germ* under the pseudonym Ellen Alleyn allegedly invented for her by her brother Dante Gabriel Rossetti. The oddity of the approximately mirrored form of the two parts of that alliterative *nom de plume* (in which an 'A' for an 'E' and the presence of an additional 'Y' jar the sight) derives also from the fact that it is clearly not a male one, which one might expect in the journal publication of a 'brotherhood'. Indeed, the pseudonym registers the distinctiveness of the poetic voice itself. Clearly, female authorship would not go unnoticed in an otherwise all male context, and Christina Rossetti was the only woman to grace the pages of *The Germ*. Moreover, in 1850, she did so with the status of a much more established poet than her brother D. G. Rossetti. If we are to understand the early visual and verbal impetus of the Pre-

Raphaelites it is important that we locate this early work within the conscious designation 'Pre-Raphaelite' and thereby situate the contents of *The Germ* in their relation to one another rather than taking Christina Rossetti out of that context because of her gender and because of the profoundly devotional nature of her verse. Isobel Armstrong has written that 'it is in Christina Rossetti's earlier poetry that her most powerful energies are at play' and in which we find 'both moments of lyric exhilaration and resilient and savage wit' (Armstrong 366). As we shall discover, these qualities are strikingly evident in those poems of hers that appear in the short-lived idiosyncratic context of the Pre-Raphaelite journal.

In that first issue of *The Germ* and on the page facing her brother's 'My Sister's Sleep' appears Christina Rossetti's 'Dream Land' in which we find in the power of the lyric moment the coming together of the states of sleep and death. I quote the poem as a whole:

> Where sunless rivers weep
> Their waves into the deep,
> She sleeps a charmed sleep;
>   Awake her not.
> Led by a single star,
> She came from very far,
> To seek where shadows are
>   Her pleasant lot.
>
> She left the rosy morn,
> She left the fields of corn,
> For twilight cold and lorn,
>   And water-springs.
> Thro' sleep, as thro' a veil,
> She sees the sky look pale,
> And hears the nightingale,
>   That sadly sings.
>
> Rest, rest, a perfect rest,
> Shed over brow and breast;
> Her face is toward the west,
>   The purple land.
> She cannot see the grain
> Ripening on hill and plain;
> She cannot feel the rain
>   Upon her hand.

Rest, rest, for evermore
Upon a mossy shore,
Rest, rest, that shall endure,
Till time shall cease; –
Sleep that no pain shall wake,
Night that no morn shall break,
Till joy shall overtake
Her perfect peace.

According to W. M. Rossetti 'Dream Land' was written in April, 1849, 'before *The Germ* was thought of', and he writes 'it may be as well to say that all my sister's contributions to this magazine were produced without any reference to publication in that or in any particular form' (*Germ* 21). Although it is true that Christina Rossetti had already published the privately printed *Verses* in 1847, and two poems in *The Athenaeum* in 1848, her brother's comment here is curious and consistent with an enduring tendency to regard her work as other than Pre-Raphaelite. For as 'Dream Land' bears witness, Christina Rossetti's early poetry, as it appears in *The Germ*, is in many ways part of an experimental aesthetic characteristic of Pre-Raphaelitism. With hindsight, Christina Rossetti's work may be said to follow a trajectory different from that of the other poets who figured in the journal, but her early poems were consistent with aspects of Pre-Raphaelite thinking as it was beginning to shape itself, such as: an emphasis on the lyric form; a propensity to privilege the corporeal by way of the verbal; a visual starkness almost hallucinatory in its concentration. The influence of Tennyson's *Poems Chiefly Lyrical* is prominent in her early work, not only for the realization of figures of women in legendary isolation, but also in terms of a singular visual imperative by which the simplest language produces profound conceptual complexities. Yet distinct from the literal and metaphorical intensity of Tennyson's 'Mariana', for example, with its alternating third and first person voices 'Dream Land' 'speaks' in a third person that strives for stark intimacy with the reader. That intimacy comes through in Rossetti's celebration of that which Hans-Georg Gadamer has termed 'a hold upon nearness'[3] peculiar to the poetic form of the lyric itself.

If we thus read in conjunction 'Dream Land' and 'My Sister's Sleep', two poems 'from one household' as they were labelled in

49

the first number of *The Germ*, their physical proximity on the page belies considerable differences in the poetic voices of their speakers. Both poems detail an outward perception of events, but Christina Rossetti's more abstract and internalized poem is concerned much less with particulars of local detail than D. G. Rossetti's verse. There is narrative surety in D. G. Rossetti's poem; Christina Rossetti's poem actively invites its absence. While in the familiar manner of Tennyson's 'Lady of Shalott', the 'she' of 'Dream Land' is framed by an external perspective vast in scope but delineated with phenomenological intensity, 'My Sister's Sleep', turns upon a series of particular domestic observations presented very much as the products of the idiosyncratic consciousness of the sibling speaker. While both poems situate the figure of a woman in death in a wider context of historical time D. G. Rossetti's poem is locked into a contemporary domestic sphere; Christina Rossetti's poem carves out a mythical open space simultaneously private and closed. 'Dream Land' further activates an external world defined wholly in relationship to an unnamed 'she' by a series of negatives that focus the sensorium: 'She cannot see the grain/Ripening on hill and plain;/She cannot feel the rain/ Upon her hand', negatives that newly devolve to the reader the senses of sight and touch. 'My Sister's Sleep' roots the event of death in the observing consciousness of a male persona and portrays a filial relationship, while 'Dream Land' evades assigning to its speaker a gendered consciousness. Indeed, the latter pares down the state of consciousness to a gentle condition of apocalypse in which 'time shall cease'.

Both poems underscore the state of sleep as portending death and play upon a slippage between the two states. The object of 'Dream Land' 'sleeps a charmed sleep' and the injunction is to 'Awake her not' where in 'My Sister's Sleep' a fear of waking the sleeping woman turns into a realization of the masking of death by sleep:

> Anxious, with softly stepping haste,
> Our mother went where Margaret lay,
> Fearing sounds o'erhead – should they
> Have broken her long-watched for rest!

Seizing the poignancy of a moment of mistaking death for sleep, of protecting the sleeping subject from disturbance, both poems explore the sudden redundancy of such protection. 'Dream Land' oddly conflates sleep as a state of heightened consciousness and 'rest' as a state devoid of sensation. A subtle slippage from the second to the third stanza renders, by way of a fine shift in season, the object's apperception of the 'pale' looking sky and the sad sound of the nightingale turned to negatives in an inability both to 'see' and to 'feel'. In this sense Rossetti recalls Wordsworth's 'A Slumber did my spirit Seal' in which the loss of the senses equates to a loss of bodily 'motion' and incorporation into the larger cosmic space: 'No motion has she now, no force;/She neither hears nor sees;/Roll'd round in earth's diurnal course,/ With rocks, and stones, and trees.'

It is revealing to compare 'My Sister's Sleep' and 'Dream Land' with poems by the sculptor, and founder member of the Pre-Raphaelites, Thomas Woolner, namely 'My Beautiful Lady' and 'Of My Lady in Death' which also appeared in that initial issue of *The Germ*. While Woolner's control of poetic structure and rhyme-scheme appear stilted, in many ways his verse is significant for its distinctive portrayal of woman as muse. Both poems manipulate the familiar courtly love convention of praising itemized physical attributes of beauty to produce a modern depiction of sexuality and obsession. Distinct, for example, from Philip Sidney's sonnet sequence *Astrophil and Stella* that maintains a distance between a platonic and a sexualized 'Ovidian' love, Woolner's poetic 'I' longs to be subsumed by the beloved. A strong impulse to surrender self is key to both poems; surrender both to the 'Lady' in life and after death. More precisely, the poems articulate a desire to achieve the inextricability of soul from body, a condition which, as we shall find, the critic Robert Buchanan heavily censured D. G. Rossetti for promoting. In truncated lines and clipped rhymes the speaker in Woolner's 'Of My Lady in Death' reflects upon his reciprocated physical 'bliss':

> By my still gaze she must have known
> The mighty bliss that filled
> My whole soul, for she thrilled,
> Drooping her face, flushed, on my own;
> I felt that it was such
> By its light warmth of touch.

The speaker recognizes a moment of perfect consummation that calls forth in retrospect 'the mute doom of death'; the poetic voice articulates, even as that moment is being experienced, the proximity of death to the moment of 'bliss'. He subsequently pours scorn upon a concept of soulmates since he must live on following the death of his beloved; death undermines, rather than affirms, a concept of the inextricability of souls:

> That body lies in cold decay,
> Which held the vital soul
> When she was my life's soul.
> Bitter mockery it was to say –
> 'Our souls are as the same:'
> My words now sting like shame;
> Her spirit went, and mine did not obey.

While Woolner's verse is clearly marked by inexperience and a forced rhyme, it visualizes the female lover in ways significant to the Pre-Raphaelites as a whole. Indeed, the poem openly prioritizes a woman's sexuality and a male speaker's dependence upon her active sexual love as a simultaneously spiritual experience. Moreover, shame is here absent in a desire for emotional and physical possession by the beloved. In this respect, Woolner's poem may be compared with William Morris' 'In Praise of My Lady' from *The Defence of Guenevere and Other Poems* (1858), the first volume of Pre-Raphaelite verse, self-consciously so in its dedication to D. G. Rossetti 'painter'.[4] Arguably, though, Woolner's comparative lack of sophistication when set alongside Morris' poem highlights more starkly the distinctive use of medievalizing attributes to articulate sexual desire.

Highly complex in these poems is the intricate expression of male self-definition through physical as well as emotional dependency upon a female other. More tellingly still, for the Pre-Raphaelites, a male subject's longing to *be* the female beloved represents a form of equivalence distinct from traditional accounts of the muse. For it is a structure of desire that frustrates a controlling poetic distance between subject and object; the desiring subject frequently collapses into the object of his or her desire to the extent that, as we will find, he or she becomes in criticism an object of derision. As Robert Buchanan memorably declared in his notorious attack upon D. G. Rossetti that we will consider below, 'D. G. Rossetti *is* "Helen of Troy", just as he *is* "Lileth". There is no separation.'[5] While D. G. Rossetti takes his models of lover and beloved from the early Italian poets, especially Dante's relation to Beatrice, he makes his own that correspondence with the beloved, inflecting it with qualities that retrospectively become incipient symbolist tendencies.

Christina Rossetti's 'An End' written in March 1849 takes the death of 'Love' as its subject and concludes the first issue of *The Germ*:

> Love, strong as death, is dead.
> Come, let us make his bed
>   Among the dying flowers:
> A green turf at his head;
> And a stone at his feet,
> Whereon we may sit
>   In the quiet evening hours.
>
> He was born in the spring,
> And died before the harvesting.
>   On the last warm summer day
>   He left us; – he would not stay
> For autumn twilight cold and grey
> Sit we by his grave and sing
>   He is gone away.
>
> To few chords, and sad, and low,
>   Sing we so.
> Be our eyes fixed on the grass,
> Shadow-veiled, as the years pass,
> While we think of all that was
>   In the long ago.

The poem charts the death of 'Love', personified as male, the preparations for his burial and subsequent gestures of mourning. While the male personification of love is a poetic commonplace, by shifts in tense and in seasonal progression Christina Rossetti subtly undermines the apparently straightforward narrative element of the verse. The opening line declares that 'Love' is newly dead, while in the subsequent portion of the stanza the speaker enjoins the auditor to fashion a grave for love 'among the dying flowers'. Already, though, by the fourth and fifth stanzas, a disruption of the natural world occurs; the turf and the stone of the grave are inverted: 'a green turf at his head;

And a stone at his feet'. Rossetti mixes a local with a cosmic view of time such that it is only at the close that the reader may interpret the chronology of the verse, recognizing the central stanza contains the song which is sung 'to few chords, and sad, and low', while the final stanza evokes the passage of time in terms of a larger retrospective moment: 'the long ago'. The collective 'we' and 'us' used throughout prevent the reader from attributing to 'Love' a simple or determinate relationship. Moreover, as is so often the case in Christina Rossetti's poems, the male pronoun is ambiguous: 'he' may refer to a male persona or to Christ in the same line. Or, here, where the pronoun refers to 'Love', it may denote human or divine love.

It is tempting with Rossetti to subordinate the human to the divine, so used are we in reading her work to privilege Christian devotion over earthly concerns. Yet, highly significant is the manner in which her poetic voice conflates the human and the divine, the 'he' as earthly lover with the 'he' as Christ, or the 'he' as variously 'Cupid' or 'Eros', thereby confounding a choice of one over the other. The deceptively difficult nature of 'An End' is signalled initially in the opening line: 'Love, strong as death, is dead.' For here the equivalence forged between love and death is unexpected, one by which 'Love', on a par with 'death', has given way to that state. While there exists perhaps optimism in this line – that for love to die is not to mourn a loss since love shares death's strength – more suggestive is the lack of correspondence between one state and the other conveyed in the proximity of noun to adjective, present to past. Indeed, the sense of the line would be quite different if without the emphatic present tense of 'is dead' it read 'love, strong as death, has died'. The effect of the alternation in the AABBBA rhyme scheme is to produce a straightforward and irrefutably declarative tone.

The second issue of *The Germ* (February 1850) contained three poems by Christina Rossetti, 'A Pause of Thought', 'Song' and 'A Testimony', the most contributions by a single author in any issue apart from W. M. Rossetti's four contributions to the final number, which, distinct from his sister's, read rather like making up the copy. 'A Pause of Thought' is a profoundly evocative poem that through the power of internal dialogue ponders abiding faith and an inability to act upon hopelessness:

I looked for that which is not, nor can be,
And hope deferred made my heart sick, in truth;
But years must pass before a hope of youth
Is resigned utterly.

I watched and waited with a steadfast will:
And, tho' the object seemed to flee away
That I so longed for, ever, day by day,
I watched and waited still.

Sometimes I said, – 'This thing shall be no more;
My expectation wearies, and shall cease;
I will resign it now, and be at peace:' –
Yet never gave it o'er.

Sometimes I said, – 'It is an empty name
I long for; to a name why should I give
The peace of all the days I have to live?' –
Yet gave it all the same.

Alas! thou foolish one, – alike unfit
For healthy joy and salutary pain,
Thou knowest the chase useless, and again
Turnest to follow it.

As Armstrong has demonstrated, Christina Rossetti's early poems 'constantly define the lyric writer as shut out, at the margin' (Armstrong 366). Throughout 'A Pause of Thought' the object of desire to which the speaker looks shifts definition, never named but denoted by various negatives. To begin with the object is 'that which is not', 'nor can be' but it alters across the second and third stanzas to become in the third 'an empty name/ I long for'. The speaker's reflection – 'to a name why should I give/The peace of all the days I have to live?' – tantalizes the reader who craves to know what the 'empty name' might denote in the context of verse which has declared its object entirely in negative terms. The final stanza, shifting in the third person to a reprimand of the speaker, provides an analogy that is simultaneously compromised in the bringing together of 'healthy joy' and 'salutary pain'. The speaker's wish to embrace excessive emotion, a surfeit of hope, undermines a common notion of the beneficial nature of a measured amount of pain. Moreover, the title 'A Pause of Thought', indicating a space or gap within thinking, hints at an expression linguistically proximate to it but one that in sentiment couldn't be at a further remove: 'a pause for thought'. The poem signals itself as pure thought, thought that has gleaned for itself a place to rest. And although 'thought' is not directly personified here as is 'Love' in the previous poem, anthropomorphism is present when she uses 'of' to denote 'belonging to', a pause which 'belongs to' thought. The verse appears reluctant to entertain an alternative interpretation of the phrase 'a pause of thought', one that might denote a space for reflection distinct from a predominant state of being in opposition to that of thought. Rather, Rossetti revels in what amounts to a tautological play upon reflection, self-reflection self-consciously performed by thought.

W. M. Rossetti claims the poem was composed in February 1848, when his sister 'was but little turned seventeen': 'Taken as a personal utterance (which I presume it to be, though I never inquired as to that, and though it was at first named "Lines in Memory of Schiller's Der Pilgrim"), it is remarkable; for it seems to show that, even at that early age, she aspired ardently after poetic fame, with a keen sense of "hope deferred".'[6] It is telling that he reads the poem primarily in terms of 'poetic fame' and, introducing Schiller as literary antecedent, attempts to divert attention from Christina Rossetti's exploration of intense desire. Not only does such a gloss seem not to adequately fit the poem, but it also belies a certain antipathy on W. M. Rossetti's part to his sister's position, a further desire to divorce her work from that of Pre-Raphaelite writers and evidence, if we needed it, of how inept a reader of her verse he was. Such interpretation refuses to situate Christina Rossetti's early poetry other than as a coherent and self-consciously determined enterprise entirely separate from Pre-Raphaelite concerns.

Christina Rossetti's 'Song' appeared in the February issue of *The Germ*:

> Oh! roses for the flush of youth,
>   And laurel for the perfect prime;
> But pluck an ivy-branch for me,
>   Grown old before my time.
>
> Oh! violets for the grave of youth,
>   And bay for those dead in their prime;
> Give me the withered leaves I chose
>   Before in the olden time.

Common to her contributions as a whole to *The Germ*, and by deceptively straightforward means, 'Song' invokes floral tributes as befitting predictable stages of life and death. Yet the rather unexpected matching in line four of 'ivy-branch' to a poetic 'I' 'grown old before [her] time', gains a further profound twist with the movement in the second stanza to the past tense: 'Give me the withered leaves I chose/Before in the olden time.' Such an abrupt temporal disjunction between the two stanzas instils a major conceptual shift between them. While the first sets the speaker's floral tribute in the context of life, with violet and rose as symbols of erotic love, the second situates it, as long already determined, in the context of premature death. The effect is to mix shock and a kind of perverse comfort in the appropriateness of 'withered leaves'. The effusiveness of the apostrophe 'Oh!' at the beginning of both stanzas heightens the musicality and declarative tone. Moreover, owing to the seemingly simple, almost nonchalant sentiment, the great passage of time conveyed by the movement of the verse is not immediately evident. The reader is thus left to speculate upon the location of that 'olden time' as juxtaposed with the joyful and undeniable symbols of youthful love.

While Christina Rossetti herself was not a painter, in her poem 'In an Artist's Studio' (1856) she realizes those ways in which the act of painting fixes the beauty of the beloved in forms as affective as 'rose' or 'violet'. She emphasizes the narcissistic identification played out in Dante Gabriel's work whereby the face of the beloved holds the symbolic plenitude of the time-honoured floral tributes of 'Song':

> One face looks out from all his canvases,
> One self-same figure sits or walks or leans:
> We found her hidden just behind those screens,
> That mirror gave back all her loveliness.
> A queen in opal or in ruby dress,
> A nameless girl in freshest summer-greens,
> A saint, an angel; – every canvas means
> The same one meaning, neither more or less.
> He feeds upon her face by day and night,
> And she with true kind eyes looks back on him,
> Fair as the moon and joyful as the light:
> Not wan with waiting, not with sorrow dim;
> Not as she is, but was when hope shone bright;
> Not as she is, but as she fills his dream.

Although the painter here fashions his model in recognizable guises, fit subjects for art – queen; girl; saint; angel – it is to the model's reciprocation of the painter's intense look that the poem seems most to want to bring its reader: 'He feeds upon her face by day and night,/And she with true kind eyes looks back on him'. This impulse to 'feed' upon the face, the face of the model, the painted face, provides a potent motif for D. G. Rossetti, one played out in *The House of Life* or as Walter Pater so knowingly called it the '"haunted" house'[7] of his sonnet sequence. In that later volume, in the 'Willowwood' series of sonnets we witness not only a familiar symbolist preoccupation with narcissistic identification in the form of reflected images in water, but also a transformation of such familiar specular structures. In the first sonnet the speaker and the figure of love sit 'upon a woodside well' and their 'mirrored' eyes meet 'silently'. As the sound of love's lute is transformed into the passionate voice of the beloved the speaker declares:

> and my tears fell.
> And at their fall, his eyes beneath grew hers;
> And with his foot and with his wing-feathers
> He swept the spring and watered my heart's drouth.
> Then the dark ripples spread to waving hair,
> And as I stooped, her own lips rising there
> Bubbled with brimming kisses at my mouth.

Here, the self-kiss of the Narcissus-like speaker occurs as a reflection in the well. The kiss and love's mournful song of death span the second and third sonnets and in the fourth – as the song dies, the kiss ends and the reflected image of the beloved falls back and is drowned – the speaker drinks in the lost image from the well in a moment of complete narcissistic identification. That identification includes the powerful physical presence of 'Love's face':

> Only I know that I leaned low and drank
> A long draught from the water where she sank,
> Her breath and all her tears and all her soul:
> And as I leaned, I know I felt Love's face
> Pressed on my neck with moan of pity and grace,
> Till both our heads were in his aureole.

But it is not only such an account of 'death' that haunts

Christina Rossetti's 'In an Artist's Studio' but also a desire for absorption, incorporation into the image of the beloved whether painted or reflected. Such recourse to the figure of Narcissus is present in D. G. Rossetti's well-known portraits of women in which we encounter the persistent compulsion to create, as a self-portrait of the artist, a woman's face. In part this preoccupation owes to the fact that the invention of photography, and its historical proximity to the development of Pre-Raphaelitism – the overt doubling that photography performs – means that painters no longer have the same compulsion to present doubles within the image. Instead, an image of a single figure may function as a type of double, and we find as a consequence paintings of the Pre-Raphaelites, and the later Symbolists, sharing with photography a compulsive relationship to processes of identification (Smith 74–94).

Such paintings as *Bocca Baciata* (1859), *Fazio's Mistress* (1863), *Lady Lileth* (1864-8), *Regina Cordium* (1866), criticized by some for sacrificing the identity of the model to an interest in woman as a sign of male creativity or of male desire, explore intricate modes of identification; ones becoming newly articulated precisely as the medium of photography alters a viewer's relationship to his or her own self-image. Rossetti's portraits of women function thus in the manner of mirror images or, post-photography, as misrecognized images of the self of the artist. They stand in relation to Rossetti as a photograph of the artist might, in the sense that they perform a doubling function. But that function is assumed in a culture in which the status of the double has altered from a seemingly knowable second self, to that 'identical' second self generated by photography. It is thus as if, post photography, a less overt double remains in the form of a more persistent type of narcissistic projection. Thus, in Rossetti's poem 'The Portrait', for example, the speaker identifies as his own mirror-reflection his painting of his beloved:

> This is her picture as she was:
>   It seems a thing to wonder on,
> As though mine image in the glass
>   Should tarry when myself am gone.

In the lines that follow we appreciate the significance of the phrase 'this is her picture as she was' (a direct echo of Robert

Browning's 'My Last Duchess') as conveying both the past of the portrait and the posthumous existence of the beloved:

> I gaze until she seems to stir,–
> Until mine eyes almost aver
> That now, even now, the sweet lips part
> To breathe the words of the sweet heart:–
> And yet the earth is over her.

The immortalization in portraiture of the dead beloved provides the context for an intense psychological exploration of the male speaker while the parting of 'the sweet lips' recalls the kissed mouth of Rossetti's painting *Bocca Baciata* (1859), whose fullness reputedly incited its patron George Boyce to repeatedly kiss the canvas: its already 'kissed' mouth. The title of that painting comes from Boccaccio's *Decameron*, second day, eighth story – 'a kissed mouth does not lose its freshness, for like the moon it always renews itself' – and some critics found Rossetti's visualization almost indecent. Regarded as one of the earliest symbolist works and indicative of the sensuality Rossetti's paintings would subsequently convey, *Bocca Baciata* is painted as if from the place of the photographic double: from that point from which one is seen by the other, but from which one can never see oneself, except in a photograph. In this, as in all of Rossetti's paintings displaying women in confined spaces, close to the picture plane, we encounter a newly insistent pursuit of such a fantasy of wholeness distinct from that given by a mirror. It is as if as viewers we look back from the depths of a mirror now transformed by the photographic image. For in restoring the age-old lateral inversion of the mirror a photograph renders perverse that earlier form of self-reflection, making all the more urgent Pre-Raphaelite painters' preoccupation with narcissism. More emphatically, those poems such as Christina Rossetti's 'In an Artist's Studio', by precisely exploring such narcissistic identification, articulate in advance that very possibility of a voice from beyond the grave that her brother D. G. Rossetti yearned for. In turn, as we shall discover, such an embodied voice reinstates the flesh in an inextricable conjunction of body and soul, best articulated in the visual and verbal pairing of *ut pictura poesis*, that peculiar state of equipoise in which painting and poem co-exist.

Although short-lived, *The Germ* was founded upon a

commitment to the aesthetic of *ut pictura poesis* with its visual and verbal interchange. As Jean Hagstrum's seminal text *The Sister Arts* reminds us, tracing the place of literary pictorialism in English poetry from Dryden to Gray, what became in the eighteenth century a very popular and fashionable phrase '*ut pictura poesis*' had been present for centuries.[8] While the critics of antiquity frequently compared poetry and painting such that for Plato in *The Republic* the poet is like a painter and for Aristotle in *The Poetics* 'painting' resembles in certain ways its 'sister' art of poetry, it was Horace who coined the now well-known phrase '*ut pictura poesis*' (Hagstrum 9). In the passage from the *Ars Poetica* in which he did so Horace argues, 'that some poems please only once but that others can bear repeated readings and close critical examination' (Hagstrum 9) and that the same is true of painting: 'As a painting, so also a poem'.[9] Yet, as David Marshall has indicated, 'Horace's original use of the words "*ut pictura poesis*"' was 'a casual comparison'; he 'did not advocate the school of thought that came to be associated with the phrase'.[10] For Hagstrum, Horace's treatise offers an account differing from those of Plato and Aristotle in so far as for Horace 'imitation meant usually either imitation of other authors, imitation of the actual conditions and customs of life, or imitation of the object as it exists in nature' (Hagstrum 10).

While Plutarch held a similar view of mimesis to Horace, he cites as a definition of the sister arts relation 'the comment which he attributed to Simonides of Ceos (c.556–467 BC), that painting is mute poetry and poetry a speaking picture' (Hagstrum 10). Although, as we have found, the Pre-Raphaelites put great aesthetic stock in Horace's faithfully rendered 'object[s] as [they] exist in nature' their work also expresses that which is implicit in the correspondence of 'mute' poem and 'speaking' picture. For what appears an equivalence – a silenced poem and an envoiced picture – is actually not so. Arguably there is more lost to poetry in such a correspondence than to painting. Whereas the concept of a 'speaking picture' retains its essential condition of visuality, while gaining a supplementary capacity of speech, that of a 'mute poem', as verse without sound, appears to undergo a more complete negation of essence. By definition, the lyric form as sung would 'suffer' the most as 'mute' poetry. More crucially, though, the idea of verse devoid of sound, paired down to the materiality of the sign, recalls that sense in which Rossetti's exhumed poems become mute material things. Once restored to view they are 'mute' by virtue of the fact that their 'sound' or aural dimension is subordinated to their physical or material presence.

Referring to 'the speechless language of the pictorial image' Gadamer writes that 'when we say that someone is "speechless" we do not mean that they have nothing to say. On the contrary, such speechlessness is really a kind of speech' (Gadamer 83). Indeed, for Gadamer one of the distinctive traits of lyric verse is its compelling presence that 'summons us what is "there" so that it is palpably near' (Gadamer 83). By extension, the aesthetic formula of *ut pictura poesis* might provide a form by which to celebrate that quality of presence that for Gadamer signals 'the truth of poetry'. Moreover, 'this self-fulfilment appears at its most mysterious in lyric poetry, where we cannot even determine the unified sense of poetic speech, as is especially the case with "pure poetry" since the time of Mallarmé' (Gadamer 83). If, in Gadamer's terms, the lyric thereby encapsulates such an 'unconditional case of untranslatability' how might we understand the function of pairing a painted work with a lyric poem? Clearly it would not be to illustrate in any crude way the visual components of the lyric form. But, on the contrary, such a pairing of lyric poem and painting would further point up a condition of suspension, thereby fixing a quality of 'nearness' as fundamentally untranslatable. As we shall find, for several Pre-Raphaelites the indeterminacy of speech in the lyric (the lack of a 'unified sense of poetic speech') works rather in the manner of bodily indeterminacy in the figure of the hermaphrodite.

However, rather than simply aspiring to balance visual and verbal forms, Pre-Raphaelite poets and painters sought to newly interrogate the relationship between them. As a result, to read the sister arts analogy in the work of the Pre-Raphaelites is more than simply to situate picture and poem in a state of equipoise; it is to fundamentally question processes of perception and understanding intrinsic to each of the individual art forms. This is especially true in those examples of a type of ekphrasis (in James Heffernan's sense of 'the verbal representation of graphic representation')[11] in which there occurs a direct correspondence between visual image (painting) and enunciation (poem). Thus, in D. G. Rossetti's 'Poems for Pictures' we don't find a parallel to classical Greek commentary on visual images. Instead we encounter a form of describing that assumes a special correspondence between visual and verbal forms. For Rossetti constantly attempts to keep painting and poem creatively in play without cultivating a desire to privilege finally one 'art' over the other: 'Picture and poem bear the same relation to each other' writes Rossetti, 'as beauty does in man and woman: the point of meeting where the two are most identical is the supreme perfection'.[12] Here in Rossetti's hesitant definition we find a curiously hermaphroditic interpretation that locates in a type of androgynous bodily beauty the ideal relation of picture and poem to each other.

Rossetti's commitment to a mutual transaction between poetry and painting was one that he gleaned from earlier artists such as Leonardo da Vinci:

> the imagination is to reality as the shadow to the body that casts it and as poetry is to painting, because poetry puts down her subjects in imaginary written characters, while painting puts down the identical reflections that the eye receives, as if they were real [...Poetry] does not like painting, impress the consciousness through the organ of sight'.[13]

Yet, as we have discovered, such aesthetic claims about the relative relationship to sight of poetry and painting are overturned by the subterranean journey of Rossetti's manuscript book whereby the perverse circumstance of the exhumation of words newly 'impress[es] the consciousness through the organ of sight'. But, providing a model for Rossetti's artistic method, Leonardo da Vinci intimates the way in which poetry and painting are mutually sustaining, the one being known through the other. Though seeming to subjugate poetry to painting such an ordering, as he recognizes, depends upon a fluctuating relationship as of shadow to body. As an ever-present mimicking of the object a shadow is controlled, as is vision, by the light it escapes yet which shapes it. Leonardo's emphasis elucidates Rossetti's preoccupation in his work with perception and the radical integration of vision, desire and writing.

However, Rossetti's more general correlation of picture and poem with beauty in man and woman is also, and perhaps more significantly, a studied reflection upon the figure of the hermaphrodite. As we shall find the hermaphrodite was central to Swinburne's poetic project and to Simeon Solomon's artistic one. For as a poetic and artistic figure it grew out of that condition of aesthetic interdependency that the Pre-Raphaelites sought, one that encapsulated the several dichotomies of body and spirit, flesh and soul, male and female, together with a language of sexual politics. It is a form of interdependency devoid of antagonism in which neither art form aspires to ascendancy over the other. Indeed, the conflict between graphic and verbal representation that, for example, Heffernan identifies in the works of Keats and Shelley is no longer at issue in the mid-nineteenth century.[14] Rather, Pre-Raphaelite works dramatize a profound sense that something approaching the most valuable aesthetic experience will arise from a conjunction that is identifiable neither as simply verbal nor visual.

Committed to an understanding of mimesis as a process of translation, D. G. Rossetti in his practice of writing sonnets to accompany pictures aspires to capture the linguistic movement or resonance of ekphrasis: an effect of constructing in words that which is always already lost as a visual image. In many instances what Rossetti signals as lost is a temporal instant or a thing that finds its linguistic 'memorial' in the sonnet form, in what he calls 'a moment's monument'. Stephen Bann in writing about D. G. Rossetti's watercolours of the 1850s has considered the sister arts analogy in terms of Rossetti's watercolour 'The Blue Closet' and William Morris's poem of the same title in which there occurs a careful balancing of picture to poem.[15] The idea of a perfect equipoise between image and text in Bann's use of translation is apt here. For, as we have found the aesthetic category of *ut pictura poesis* captures a state of suspension in which neither the visual nor the linguistic (picture or poem) is subject to interpretation beyond the gesture of saying to use Horace's coinage: 'as a painting, so a poem'. Such a movement is quite different from that maintaining the resemblance of one thing to another in the sense in which *ut pictura poesis* is often read: a mediation of one mode through another. For, it is an attempt to sustain a careful balancing without resolving it.

4

D. G. Rossetti's paired works

In Pre-Raphaelite poetry and painting a concept of poetic distance is precisely complicated by frequent recourse to paired works in the form of poems and paintings that rely upon a kind of redundant ekphrastic gesture, redundant in the sense that the visual artefact described in a poem is not lost to sight but remains to be seen and matched with its verbal counterpart or ekphrasis. In a context of paired works that focus desire in relation to dead female subjects, 'The Blessed Damozel' remains perhaps the best known of Rossetti's poems. It is also distinctive since the poem preceded the painting; usually Rossetti worked from painting to poem. He claimed to have written it before he was nineteen, 'inspired by the Gothickry of Poe's Lenore and The Raven': 'I saw that Poe had done the utmost it was possible to do with the grief of the lover on earth,' he said in 1882, 'and so I determined to reverse the conditions and give utterance to the yearning of the loved one in heaven'.[1] Thereby, in conceiving the poem Rossetti shifts the expression of desire from a melancholy male lover to a dead female beloved. In 'The Blessed Damozel' a concept of poetic 'doubleness', as Armstrong, (Armstrong 13–14) has expressed it, emerges in the combination of a third person, speaking for the dead woman, with some first person utterance of her desire for her living beloved to come to her.

First published in *The Germ* in 1850, later revised for his volume *Poems* (1870), Rossetti's 'most anthologised "signature poem"' was influenced especially by his namesake Dante, whose *Vita Nuova*, which Rossetti translated into English, he adopted as a text of personal import, supplying repeated inspiration for drawings and paintings. The first version is superior to the second in its evocation of an extreme physiological sense combined with a profound philosophical abstraction:

> The blessed Damozel leaned out
> From the gold bar of Heaven:
> Her blue grave eyes were deeper much
> Than a deep water, even.
> She had three lilies in her hand,
> And the stars in her hair were seven.

The difficulty of rhythm in the third and fourth lines, the jarring effect of 'even' together with those adjectives connoting naturalism, 'blue grave eyes' is enhanced by the subsequent symbolic register of lilies and stars. For the reader is forever impelled to read as 'grey' the 'grave' eyes of line three while grasping the aptness of the meanings of 'grave' as in both 'serious' and 'from beyond life'. Stanzas five and six, by comparison, shift the focus from the Damozel's face to an astronomical perspective:

Stanza 5
> It was the terrace of God's house
> That she was standing on, –
> By God built over the sheer depth
> In which Space is begun;
> So high, that looking downward thence,
> She could scarce see the sun.

Stanza 6
> It lies from Heaven across the flood
> Of ether, as a bridge.
> Beneath, the tides of day and night
> With flame and blackness ridge
> The void, as low as where this earth
> Spins like a fretful midge

The Darwinian resonance of 'this earth spin[ning] like a fretful midge' combines with a primeval metaphysical voice to create a conjoined Biblical and evolutionary space. By incorporating scientific discourse, Rossetti's poem also corresponds with Tennyson's *In Memoriam* of the same year in which poetic expression of mourning is inseparable from discourses of geology and astronomy. At the same time, overt echoes of Tennyson's 'Mariana' crystallize in the eleventh stanza: ' "I wish that he were come to me,/ For he will come," she said', though 'the Blessed Damozel's' refrain turns around Mariana's and is distinguished by its positive questioning of the body/soul relation. In a very curious sense 'The Blessed Damozel' not only prefigures Siddal's death but, more emphatically, it foreshadows D. G. Rossetti's desire for communion with the dead beloved. Indeed, the poem stages the scenario of wished for communion from the grave that, as we've found, Rossetti would later both aspire to realize and also attempt to justify. Here, the reversed scenario of the dead woman pining from heaven for her earthly lover comprises an odd mix of the ethereal with the fervently physiological. Yet critical comments that highlight the oddity of the poet's reference, in the conditional tense, to the warmth of the Damozel's bosom fail to register the larger physiological context that the poem conjures in the midst of the metaphysical; Rossetti questions how one might portray a dead woman who possesses the agency of a desiring subject.

It is a poetic method congruent with that of Christina Rossetti who arguably uses it more compellingly in a poem such as 'After Death'. Both poems articulate female desire from the grave but the wishful thinking on the part of D. G. Rossetti's 'Blessed Damozel' contrasts significantly with the severity and resentment voiced by the dead woman of his sister's 'After Death', from *Goblin Market and Other Poems*, composed in 1849. Christina Rossetti creates dead subjects who are most significantly speaking subjects:

> The curtains were half drawn, the floor was swept
> And strewn with rushes, rosemary and may
> Lay thick upon the bed in which I lay,
> Where thro' the lattice ivy-shadows crept.
> He leaned above me, thinking that I slept
> And could not hear him; but I heard him say:
> 'Poor child, poor child:' and as he turned away
> Came a deep silence, and I knew he wept.
> He did not touch the shroud, or raise the fold
> That hid my face, or take my hand in his,
> Or ruffle the smooth pillows for my head:
> He did not love me living; but once dead
> He pitied me; and very sweet it is
> To know he still is warm tho' I am cold.

Moving through a string of negatives the poem performs wishful thinking on the part of the speaker: 'he did not', 'he did not' as unfulfilled wishes and desires are simultaneously made present through naming: knowable in death. As the speaker substitutes pity for love and reads as the sign of the mourner's weeping 'a deep silence', Rossetti creates an uncanny tone shifting between assurance and delusion. Critics have speculated upon the relationship of the 'he' to the dead speaker, offering most often the figure of lover or father.[2] For here in Rossetti we have the ambiguous male pronoun, coupled with the rather emphatic claim: 'He did not love me living', suggesting intense desire frustrated. Although the final sentiment as articulated in 'how sweet it is to know...' may ring ultimately as 'true' altruism or, as some critics have suggested, bitter resentment, throughout the poem a yearning to be looked at, and indeed touched, in death, here spoken by a body from beneath the shroud, anticipates a formula that resonates throughout Pre-Raphaelite works especially those of D. G. Rossetti. This formula does not simply voice a desire for a dead beloved but also, as we shall find later in Maurice Blanchot's sense of the Eurydice myth, the longed for paradox of seeing a woman with 'the fullness of her death living in her' (Blanchot 100).

For D. G. Rossetti the poetic form of the sonnet provided his preferred vehicle when twinning poem with picture. He used the Petrachan form with the standard fourteen lines delivered in iambic pentameter with an ABBA CDCDCD rhyme scheme, the octave and sestet forming distinct sections. Moreover, in addition to his individual sonnets for pictures, his sequence *The House of Life* celebrated the sonnet form. In formal terms the sonnet sequence may appear to contradict the seamless economy of the discrete sonnet; each individual sonnet is a self-contained artefact yet, set in a sequential form, assumes a different fabric through the twin presence of dependency and discreteness. Similarly, the combination of sonnet and picture establishes an interdependency between visual and verbal media whereby the sonnet as supplementary to the picture is reconfigured as both less and more than supplementary, and vice versa. That is to say, the picture holds meaning without its linguistic complement the presence of which radically reworks its unitary status. The same is differently true of the poem that, voicing visual things, does not require them for its meaning. Rossetti's favoured phrase for such a poem, 'composed for the painting,' suggests an intimate connection between image and text in the sense of a poem's having been produced 'for the pleasure or purpose of' the painting and not simply as its intermedial complement.

More generally for D. G. Rossetti, however, in the compelling though troubled relation of image to text there is a sense in which the original visual artefact subsequently articulated in the sonnet has already been lost in the act of painting; as if the very act of painting itself renders the object lost. Indeed, as we shall find, Rossetti is driven to repeat visual images, not simply approximate types of female figures but the same individual figures. Most notable of these is the image of Dante's Beatrice together with the tragic mythological figure of Proserpine who, as we shall find, by a deft sleight of hand leads to Eurydice. Rossetti produced many paired works that hold a significant place in his *oeuvre*, most notably ones in which as Jerome McGann explains 'he executes a picture and then writes a poem – typically a sonnet [...] that comments and elaborates upon the pictorial work' (*RA*). For McGann 'each part of the double work is a unique view of an ideal visionary reality whose existence is posited through the different incarnate forms' such that 'the whole of the double work becomes, then, a dynamic representation of the process by which the visionary imagination sustains and develops itself' (*RA*). Moreover, Rossetti's practice of twinning paintings and poems must be read in the context of his lifelong sense that his true vocation lay in poetry, that painting by which he made his living was an inferior art and one that he had finally prostituted himself to.

Yet how might we judge Rossetti's claim that painting, as he executed it, was ultimately for him a lesser intellectual and spiritual pursuit than poetry? Should we take Rossetti at his word? If so, how should we interpret those works which are so clearly interdependent? Profoundly influenced by William Blake's 'composite art', for McGann, Rossetti develops more obviously than does Blake what he calls 'the gap that stands between the composite parts of the double work' (*RA*). Furthermore, McGann maintains that even when 're-doubled' as in the case of *Proserpine*, Rossetti's individual works participate in dialectical relationships whereby 'the integrity of the individual elements is scrupulously preserved' within what he calls the poet's and painter's 'larger confederated set of imaginings'. By comparison, Richard Stein reminds us, as far back as 1970, that since reading Rossetti's poetry in terms of his painting has 'become so mechanically commonplace it is easy to misjudge its critical usefulness', yet he goes on to claim that the *The House of Life* demonstrates that 'the double metier again and again became a symbol of his most intense conflicts'[3], conflicts played out at both an aesthetic and personal level.

We have already touched upon the painting *Venus Verticordia*. Let's now return to that canvas in its paired relationship with the poem:

> Venus Verticordia
> (For a picture)
> She hath the apple in her hand for thee,
>   Yet almost in her heart would hold it back;
>   She muses, with her eyes upon the track
> Of that which in thy spirit they can see.
> Haply, 'Behold, he is at peace,' saith she;
>   'Alas! The apple for his lips, – the dart
>   That follows its brief sweetness to the heart, –
> The wandering of his feet perpetually!'
>
> A little space her glance is still and coy;
>   But if she give the fruit that works her spell,
> Those eyes shall flame as for her Phrygian boy.
>   Then shall her bird's strained throat the woe foretell,
>   And her far seas moan as a single shell,
> And her grove glow with love-lit fires of Troy.

The sonnet appears within the composition 'pinned as it were to the trellis, identifying the goddess of Love as a personification of the physical desire that arouses, enslaves and destroys men' (Marsh 277). Rather than appearing inscribed on the frame, a practice Rossetti frequently adopted, the sonnet thus has a physical presence as 'illuminated' within the composition. Located within the visual space of the painting the poem registers both linguistically and pictorially maintaining a form of suspension crucial to the effect desired. In part, it describes the visual scene of the painting: 'She hath the apple in her hand for thee,' but it also assigns motives to the goddess: 'Yet almost in her heart would hold it back.' Moreover, the sestet evokes the complex anterior future tense in the 'love-lit fires of Troy'. Such ekphrasis embellishes the plastic rendering of Venus but its narrative plenitude is differently figured for Swinburne, for example, in his response to Rossetti's particular painting of a patch of 'green'.

Reviewing *Venus Verticordia* in *Notes on the Royal Academy Exhibition*, 1868, Swinburne notes especially 'the painting of leaf and fruit and flower' which he claims 'is beyond my praise of any man's'.[4] 'But', he continues:

> of one thing I will take note; the flash of green brilliance from the upper leaves of the trellis against the sombre green of the trees behind. Once more it must appear that the painter alone can translate into words as perfect as music and colour the sense and spirit of his work.[5]

For Swinburne, 'the flash of green brilliance' is a translation on a par with the sovereign form of music in conveying the 'spirit' of Rossetti's work; on a par with the types of temporal fullness that the poetic allusion to the future may render. Here, the sheer material presence of paint aspires to a condition of immateriality just as the concrete presence of language in the sonnet hovers simultaneously as linguistic sign and visual image. Such qualities derive from the juxtaposition of word and image.

By contrast, the later Syrian Venus, *Astarte Syriaca* (1877) is often considered along with *Proserpine* to embody Rossetti's earlier incipient symbolist tendencies. Commissioned by Clarence Fry in 1877, according to the artist it depicts 'the Syrian Venus with ministering spirits'. Astarte was worshipped both as the incarnation of the spirit of God and as the mother of mankind. Bringing closer the ekphrastic relationship a specially designed frame, according to Rossetti's usual practice, contained the sestet of the sonnet composed for the painting, printed in full in April 1877 in *The Athenaeum*. In the colossal format of *Astarte Syriaca*, Venus confronts the viewer with physical proportions larger than those of a human form; faced with the sheer physicality of the figure he or she is impelled to identify with her. The encounter Rossetti creates for a viewer raises the spectre of doubling that he explored more overtly in images such as *How They Met Themselves*:

> Mystery! lo! betwixt the sun and moon
>   Astarte of the Syrians: Venus Queen
>   Ere Aphrodite was. In silver sheen
> Her twofold girdle clasps the infinite boon
> Of bliss whereof the heaven and earth commune:
>   And from her neck's inclining flower-stem lean
>   Love-freighted lips and absolute eyes that wean
> The pulse of hearts to the spheres' dominant tune.
>
> Torch-bearing, her sweet ministers compel
>   All thrones of light, beyond the sky and sea
>   The witnesses of Beauty's face to be:
> That face, of Love's all-penetrative spell,
> Amulet, talisman, and oracle, –
>   Betwixt the sun and moon a mystery.

In the sestet that focuses 'Beauty's face to be' we encounter the anterior future tense in a form similar to that in *Venus Verticordia* that *will* produce 'amulet, talisman and oracle', charms and divine agencies by which extraordinary results are achieved. But 'that face' as 'oracle' here is also the seat of utterance; it is not simply to be looked at – it *is* the locus of language. Again Rossetti brings to the fore a subtle interdependency of picture and poem. As with the mysterious temporal power of photography there is a key attraction for Rossetti in the painter's second sight: for the painter to 'speak' the incipient beauty of the future as it were. We return once more to the face, to the plenitude of a woman's face; invited to look into 'that face': 'amulet, talisman, and oracle'.

The compulsion to look at, to look into a face, and its significance to Rossetti, is played out in one intriguing double work, *Aspecta Medusa*, that exists without its intended visual pairing, though a pencil drawing survives. In 1867 Rossetti secured a commission from C. P. Mathews the brewer to paint Perseus and Andromeda with the severed head of the gorgon Medusa. However, he did not produce the oil painting since according to W. M. Rossetti 'Mathews reneged when he saw the finished drawing because he found the severed head repulsive'.[6] The poem thus describes the design that never came to full fruition. In this sense, relating to an absent original (here one never fully realized), the poem comes closer to the original Greek meaning of ekphrasis than many other literary works whose visual counterparts survive. Or, put differently, the poem articulates a visual project in process: that very quality to which all such paired works aspire.

> Aspecta Medusa
> Andromeda, by Perseus saved and wed,
> Hankered each day to see the Gorgon's head:
> Till o'er a fount he held it, bade her lean,
> And mirrored in the wave was safely seen
> That death she lived by.
> Let not thine eyes know
> Any forbidden thing itself, although
> It once should save as well as kill: but be
> Its shadow upon life enough for thee.

Aspecta Medusa represents an interdiction proscribing the act of looking directly at 'any forbidden thing'. In the much-represented legend of the Medusa if any one perceived the gorgon directly he or she was turned to stone. For Perseus, his polished shield provided a reflective surface by which to look indirectly at the Medusa and thereby destroy her. In Rossetti's poem and drawing Perseus, in holding the Medusa's head above a 'fount' of water, creates a safe condition in which Andromeda might see 'that death she lived by'. According to McGann the idea was entirely Rossetti's that 'Andromeda desired to see the head of the monstrous woman slain by Perseus' *(RA)*; Rossetti's invention in this regard prompts us to question such a desire to 'look upon death'. As we shall find, Rossetti's distinctive rendering of the myth echoes in fascinating terms that of Orpheus and Eurydice, especially in the injunction: 'Let not thine eyes know/Any forbidden thing itself'. For Orpheus the 'shadow upon life' was not 'enough', and he was compelled to disobey the injunction *not* to 'look' at his beloved Eurydice. In both cases, the desire of the beholder to 'look' is a desire to look *at* 'death'. One encounters within an aesthetic all about looking – in which the primary urge is to look upon death – the tremendous power held in the injunction *not* to look.

It is thereby somewhat ironic that Rossetti's patron rejected the commission on the grounds of finding the head repulsive. For the 'forbidden thing' itself was precisely intended to be visually threatening. Moreover, the enduring fascination of the Orpheus/ Eurydice myth resides to some extent in the seeming simplicity of that very injunction 'not to look'. For Orpheus has only to obey an apparently straightforward command in order to get Eurydice back. Yet that most simple action of averting the eyes proves impossible for him to perform, in spite of the fact that sight is a sense that may be controlled, unlike hearing, for example, which Ruskin pointed out could not simply be turned off at will. Herein lies part of the fascination of the myth for generations of poets and painters: how to represent in a visual medium the act of looking back at death. We will consider further this fascination but first let's examine Robert Buchanan's much-cited review of Rossetti's volume *Poems* (1870) since it initiates a chain of response to Pre-Raphaelitism more generally, one the movement struggled to shake off and one rooted in Buchanan's knowledge of the 'resurrected' poems and their aesthetic of death.

5

'The Fleshly School' Controversy

In 1871 under the pseudonym of Thomas Maitland, Robert Buchanan launched his now notorious attack on D. G. Rossetti entitled 'The Fleshly School of Poetry' in *The Contemporary Review*. [1] As Marsh indicates, Rossetti had been worried about such an attack when, having exhumed the 'lost' poems, he published them along with others as *Poems* in 1870, but 'after eighteen months of good reviews and healthy sales', it would appear to have 'had little power to injure' (Marsh 432). However, at the same time Rossetti was intrigued to know the identity of its author and felt sure it would prove to be an old 'bogey' and rival poet Robert Buchanan. Rossetti thus planned a response entitled 'The Stealthy School of Criticism, A Letter to Robert Buchanan Esq. (alias Thomas Maitland)',[2] while Buchanan expanded his original piece into a pamphlet *The Fleshly School of Poetry and Other Phenomena of the Day* issued on Rossetti's birthday. The expanded version that covered the theme of indecency more generally and dealt with visual as well as print media tipped Rossetti over the edge. His mental health had been vulnerable, and he was finally unable to withstand the implications of Buchanan's review. For as well as an individual attack it was an assault upon the Pre-Raphaelite investment in *ut pictura poesis* that for Buchanan denoted an aesthetic theory inseparable from the figure of the hermaphrodite and the dangers of effeminacy. While directing most of its vitriol to Rossetti the review also criticized Morris, Swinburne and Solomon; Buchanan approached them collectively for what he considered the sexual transgressions of their works.

In his vehement critique Buchanan called *The Germ* 'an

unwholesome periodical' (Buchanan 340). Even allowing for his characteristic wordplay in the obvious linking of wholesome-ness (in the organic metaphor) of the periodical's title, this remains a perplexing statement. What might have been Buchanan's motives in linking in this way the early poetic contents of *The Germ* with Rossetti's later poetry? What preoccupations of Rossetti's later poetry are evident in those pieces he published in *The Germ*? Andrea Rose in her facsimile edition[3] maintains that Buchanan's statement is 'undeserved' since a great deal in the periodical maintains a moral message for fine art, but more interesting is his motivation in making such a comment. In the context of the review as a whole, for Buchanan to position *The Germ* as morally suspect is an attempt to foreclose debate on what had been by 1871 a profound influence of Pre-Raphaelitism upon British Art. What is frequently referred to as the second phase of the movement was well underway by this point in time. Indeed, William Morris and Edward Burne-Jones were established figures, who had espoused, and were proudly continuing to stress, the influence of the PRB not only upon their literary and artistic practices but also upon their decisions to enter art in the first place. More crucially, in Morris' and Burne-Jones' reflections upon key influences on their work, Ruskin figures prominently as integral to a Pre-Raphaelite project. Moreover, Buchanan's review not only refers to incipient unwholesomeness in early Pre-Raphaelite poetry but to its emergence in an interdisciplin-ary context. By extension, as we shall find, for Buchanan an attack on Pre-Raphaelite investment in *ut pictura poesis* is inseparable from the literary and artistic figure of the hermaph-rodite.

Central to Buchanan's critique of *The Germ* is the suggestion that the journal promoted poetic identity premised upon subversive sexual personae:

> The fleshly gentlemen have bound themselves by solemn league and covenant to extol fleshliness as the distinct and supreme end of poetic thought, and by inference that the body is greater than the soul, and sound superior to sense; and that the poet, properly to develop his poetic faculty, must be an intellectual hermaphrodite, to whom the very facts of day and night are lost in a whirl of aesthetic terminology (Buchanan 335).

For Buchanan to privilege what he perceives as 'body' over 'soul' as equivalent to a preference for sound over sense is curious, but perhaps less so when we consider the history and impact of Rossetti's volume of poems. Here, in employing the term 'hermaphrodite', Buchanan is taking up Swinburne's use of the word in his *Notes on Poems and Reviews* (1866) written following the controversy that surrounded the publication of his *Poems and Ballads* in the same year.[4] Buchanan is also critical of a surfeit of aesthetic 'terminology', suggesting the Pre-Raphaelites have lost touch with the pragmatics of every day language. On the one hand he accuses Rossetti, and by association his group, of an over attention to base instincts, to a heightened materiality of body at the expense of soul, while on the other he berates him for his rarefied aesthetic: a language far removed from the everyday. Thus, Buchanan contradicts himself in constructing Rossetti as at once too earthy and too abstract, while his recourse to 'intellectual hermaphroditism' interestingly blurs accepted intellectual as well as sexual distinctions.

Yet, it is significant that in spite of all his claims to the contrary there existed some truth for Rossetti in Buchanan's charge of 'fleshliness'. To be sure Rossetti laboured to avert the realization that the body and soul dichotomy that he so longed to refute threatened constantly to assail him. Moreover, Buchanan's attack becomes newly meaningful in the context of the retrieval of the poems we considered above. Rossetti's extreme response to Buchanan's negative review, and his earlier attempts to control the review process by assigning reviews to his friends and supporters, begin to make sense in the context of Rossetti's guilt over the exhumation. Indeed, Buchanan's accusation of Rossetti's separation of body and soul registered all the more painfully in the light of the unorthodox extra-textual life of the volume. It was as if Buchanan articulated in barely disguised code Rossetti's unspeakable secret. What is more, his 'Fleshly School' review has assumed such notoriety in literary criticism because its vitriolic attack went to the heart of the Pre-Raphaelite project as a whole and to those elements that presented easy targets for derision such as the psychosexual content of poems and paintings.

While, those extracts that tend to be quoted denigrate Rossetti as a poet, emphasizing his portrayal of sexual love in verse pronounced devoid of talent, one of the most interesting qualities of the piece is the way it brings into play diverse aspects of Rossetti's work; almost in spite of himself Buchanan draws out of the poetry a figurative language enabling in ways contrary to his intention. Consider, for example, his use of the figure of still water to describe the poet's psyche:

> the mind of Mr Rossetti is like a glassy mere, broken only by the dive of some water-bird or the hum of winged insects, and brooded over by an atmosphere of insufferable closeness, with a light blue sky above it, sultry depths mirrored within it, and a surface so thickly sown with water-lilies that it retains its glassy smoothness even in the strongest wind (Buchanan 337).

Here, the extended metaphor of water produces a way into Rossetti's poetry according to its own figurative singularity. For Rossetti is endlessly fascinated by the mirroring qualities of reflective surfaces, particularly water, and by the doubling of the human form as in *How They Met Themselves*. This latter picture Rossetti executed on honeymoon in Paris in 1860, re-fashioning an earlier (now lost) drawing of the subject of the doppleganger from 1850.[5] Doomed lovers realize their fate when in a wood they confront their own uncanny doubles. And over a period of years Rossetti reworked the topic that became something of a compulsive theme. The image not only reiterates a preoccupation with doubling to be found in many Pre-Raphaelite works, but it also invokes the larger doubling project of the aesthetic of *ut picture poesis*.

Throughout, Buchanan's review points up a fascinating and persistent feature of Rossetti's project, namely the narcissistic relationship of the poet/painter to his creations. This preoccupation also elaborates the prominence of the figure of the hermaphrodite. Buchanan writes that '[Rossetti] is "heaven-born Helen, Sparta's queen," whose "each twin breast is an apple sweet;"[. . .] he is "Sister Helen" melting her waxen man; he is all of these, just as surely as he is Mr Rossetti soliloquising over Jenny in her London Lodging, or the very nuptial person writing erotic sonnets to his wife' (Buchanan 339). Such sexual interchangeability bothers Buchanan yet, even though he regards it in an entirely negative light, this identification between Rossetti and his female creations is a theoretically productive one. By way of such gender switches, whereby the male speaker approximates the female object of desire or of speech, Rossetti the poet approximates Swinburne's figure of the hermaphrodite as trivialized by Buchanan. Such a collapse of gender distinctions marks out not only a characteristic quality of his work, but also the modernity of Rossetti's visual and verbal project. The male artist's identification with a female subject is not simply a version of the conventional character of the muse. For Rossetti to identify with female personae is to approximate the aesthetic condition of *ut pictura poesis*, but to new ends.

For the Pre-Raphaelites more generally the classical convention of *ut pictura poesis* allows for a particular emergence of figure of the hermaphrodite. That figure of course signals the influence of French writing, most notably Baudelaire's poetry as made known to Rossetti by Swinburne who himself identified with the female figure of the ancient poet Sappho.[6] Informing Buchanan's entire review is a notion that Rossetti should have known better, a sentiment established early on in the piece in a comparison of Rossetti with Swinburne in which Swinburne as a 'little boy letting off squibs' (Buchanan 338) is exonerated for his harmlessness whereas Rossetti is without excuse owing to his maturity. We will discuss the place of Swinburne shortly but first let us consider Rossetti's response to Buchanan's attack.

The effect upon Rossetti's mental health of Buchanan's critique would prevent him from taking further poetic risks. In response to Buchanan's fierce critique Rossetti published 'The Stealthy School of Criticism' in *The Athenaeum* on 16 December 1871. The piece systematically takes up each of Buchanan's objections to demonstrate that nowhere does he 'aver that poetic expression is greater than poetic thought; and, by implication, that the body is greater than the soul, and sound superior to sense'. In levelling against Rossetti these charges Buchanan had transferred to him his earlier response to Swinburne's work. As a result of his review, a notion of 'sound' overriding 'sense' has persisted in criticism of Swinburne's verse and, one might say, in Pre-Raphaelite poetry as a whole. Rossetti shows how by taking individual lines out of context Buchanan achieves his partial reading.

On the issue of 'Jenny', one of the poems retrieved from the grave, Rossetti's comments show the extent to which the text had remained for him significant precisely because of its sexually and morally provocative subject matter:

> Neither some thirteen years ago, when I wrote this poem, nor last year when I published it, did I fail to foresee impending charges of recklessness and aggressiveness, or to perceive that even some among those who could really *read* the poem, and acquit me on these grounds, might still hold that the thought in it had better have dispensed with the situation which serves it for framework.[...] But the motive powers of art reverse the requirement of science, and demand first of all an *inner* standing-point. The heart of such a mystery as this must be plucked from the very world in which it beats or bleeds; and the beauty and pity, the self-questionings and all-questionings which it brings with it, can come with full force only from the mouth of one alive to its whole appeal, such as the speaker put forward in the poem, – that is, of a young and thoughtful man of the world. To such a speaker, many half-cynical revulsions of feeling and reverie, and a recurrent presence of the impressions of beauty (however artificial) which first brought him within such a circle of influence, would be inevitable features of the dramatic relations portrayed.[7]

The nature of Rossetti's defence here, acknowledging the transgressive potential of his subject matter, coupled with a commitment to achieve a depth of psychological realism in the self-conscious creation of personae, also motivates his creation of the speaker in 'A Last Confession' and his defence of the vilified 'harlot's laugh' from that poem. But additionally it is a line of defence that Swinburne had used in 1866 to counter John Morley's attack on his own poems. The poetic creation of personae was indeed a common device, used extensively by Browning, Tennyson and Arnold. But in spite of such bold precedents, Rossetti's and Swinburne's personae aroused deep suspicion such that Rossetti's speaker in 'Jenny' might prove more offensive than Browning's in 'Porphyria's Lover'.

One premise that inflects Buchanan's opinion overall in 'The Fleshly School' is that the sister arts analogy, that we have previously considered, the mutually informing and dependent relationship between poem and painting, is essentially a flawed and dangerous one. And even though he cites the example of 'The Blessed Damozel' as having 'great merits of its own, and a few lines of real genius' (Buchanan 340) Buchanan objects to it as a poem twinned with a painting: as a 'double work'. Yet offended as he is by 'doubling' it is not because he believes one art form renders another redundant. He writes:

The truth is that literature, and more particularly poetry, is in a very bad way when one art gets hold of another, and imposes upon it its conditions and limitations. In the first few verses of the Damozel we have the subject, or part of the subject, of a picture, and the inventor should either have painted it or left it alone altogether; and, had he done the latter, the world would have lost nothing. Poetry is something more than painting; and an idea will not became a poem because it is too smudgy for a picture. (Buchanan 340)

Buchanan tellingly reads the sister arts analogy as a type of carnal relation whereby 'one art gets hold of the other' to impose itself upon it. Thereby, he entirely misrepresents Rossetti's attempt to balance the translation of one medium into another. Buchanan's predictably Platonic privileging of poetry over painting emerges out of a rather simplistic notion that, more than poetry, painting belongs with concrete ideas. Yet in what sense in the period in which Buchanan is writing might poetry be said to be '*more* than painting' in the way that he describes? He confidently pronounces the beginning of 'The Blessed Damozel' more suited to the visual than the verbal arts and, thereby, to counteract its transgressive possibilities, rejects *ut pictura poesis* as a viable aesthetic position together with the poetic power of ekphrasis. Further undermining his argument, he employs the metaphor 'smudgy' evocative of the graphic arts to designate an idea lacking concrete form. Buchanan announces a form of doubling as offensive, vehemently opposing ways in which he claims painting can obtrude 'nasty' unmanly private sensations.

It is little wonder that when William Morris published *The Defence of Guenevere* volume in 1858 ('dedicated to my friend Rossetti') critics should regard it as displaying the worst excesses of Pre-Raphaelitism: its 'absurdities and extravagances'. Indeed, Morris' first volume of poetry caused reviewers such as John Skelton to claim that 'for myself, I am sick of Rossetti and his whole school. I think them essentially unmanly, effeminate, mystical, affected, and obscure'.[8] Characteristically, what were identified as Pre-Raphaelite conditions of effeminacy in Morris'

Defence and Henry Wallis' *Chatterton* in the 1850s find their full expression in the 1860s and 70s not only in the poetry and painting of Rossetti but also the poetry of Swinburne and the painting of Solomon.

SWINBURNE: THE PERVERSITY OF THE HERMAPHRODITE

That Buchanan finds it difficult to separate Rossetti's verse from his painting is to some extent a measure of Rossetti's success: the perfect slippage or translation of one medium into the other, words into paint. However, in larger terms, it strategically downplays the interests of Pre-Raphaelite poets and painters by attempting to rid them of any possible political critique. In drawing up a series of idiosyncratic traits common to the poets, Buchanan's review is thereby instructive for its overarching vision of Pre-Raphaelitism. It is one in which the so-called second generation, most obviously Swinburne and Morris, though relegated to walk on roles in Buchanan's imagined scenario of *Hamlet*, are inseparable from the first generation, most notably Rossetti, as the malign centre to which they gravitate. Rossetti has long been recognized as the enduring spirit of early through late Pre-Raphaelitism while at the same time being portrayed as atypical. Yet his work is not atypical. Morris' *The Defence of Guenevere* has a different emphasis but the same visual and verbal force is present there. Swinburne's poems are distinct from Rossetti's but they embody similar aesthetic concerns including, as we shall find, a preoccupation with bodily indeterminacy. In this context Buchanan's purpose in thus relegating to a position below that of Rossetti, Swinburne's potential for infecting the public, appears strategic: an attempt to divert attention from those larger contraventions implicit in earlier responses to his poetry.

The well-known reviews of Swinburne's *Poems and Ballads* (1866), including the vituperative critique by John Morley in *The Saturday Review* (1866), find Swinburne's sexual subject matter outrageous for its lack of moral responsibility. Morley's damning piece casts Swinburne as ultimately irredeemable and his own desire to change his poetic interests futile: 'what comes of discoursing to a fiery tropical flower of the pleasant fragrance of

82

the rose or the fruitfulness of the fig-tree'.[9] As a poet, then, Swinburne has neither the refinement of an English sensibility nor the fecundity of a southern one as represented by the fig. Instead he labours in a 'barren' field. What is more, Morley's metaphor of sterility is inseparable from the charges of excessive sensuality and effeminacy that he levels against the poet: 'It is not every poet who would ask us all to go hear him tuning his lyre in a stye. It is not everybody who would care to let the world know that he found the most delicious food for poetic reflection in the practices of the great island of the Aegean, in the habits of Messalina, of Faustina, of Pasiphae.'[10]

In his defence, Swinburne offered a theory of poetry that redrew the parameters of the art form, re-establishing a distance between the identity of the poet and those personae he created. Following the powerful use of the dramatic monologue form by Browning and Tennyson, Swinburne separated himself from his 'perverse' creations: 'the book is dramatic, many-faced, multifarious; and no utterance of enjoyment or despair, belief or unbelief, can properly be assumed as the assertion of its author's personal feeling or faith'.[11] Of the maligned poem 'Delores' he writes:

> I have striven here to express the transient state of spirit through which a man may be supposed to pass, foiled in love and weary of loving, but not yet in sight of rest; seeking refuge in those 'violent delights' which have 'violent ends', in fierce and frank sensualities which at least profess to be no more than they are. This poem, like *Faustine*, is so distinctly symbolic and fanciful that it cannot justly be amenable to judgement as a study in the school of realism.[12]

Stevenson cites the occasion upon which, ahead of the publication of *Poems and Ballads* and in order to 'test the moral impact of the poems, [Swinburne] read most of the manuscript one evening to Ruskin, and was "sincerely surprised by the enjoyment he seemed to derive from [his] work, and the frankness with which he accepted it"'.[13] And Stevenson reminds us how Ruskin wrote the next day 'anxiously to Swinburne's most trusted woman friend Lady Trevelyan: "I heard [...] some of the wickedest and splendidest verse ever written by a human creature. He drank three bottles of porter while I was there. I don't know what to do with him or for him, but he mustn't publish these things"'.[14] As it turned out, the abuse received by *Poems and Ballads* in 1866 prior to its publication in July caused the publisher Moxon to withdraw it from the market in August. Following 'negotiations and threats of legal proceedings, the edition was transferred to a less reputable publisher John Camden Hotten who was happy to take advantage of the scandal that the reviews and the suppression had propagated'.[15]

As Karen Alkalay-Gut has pointed out 'since their publication, the contents of *Poems and Ballads* has been considered problematic because of the representation of perverse sexuality in prosodically assured forms that seem uninterested in any moral framework'.[16] Moreover, critics found especially disconcerting this perceived mismatch between assured prosody (poetic sophistication in the extreme) and outrageous subject matter. In Swinburne's verse the dimensions of sound and sense which as Gadamer reminds us are 'inextricably interwoven' in poetry reach 'in some forms of linguistic art an extreme point where they become totally indissoluble [...] where we confront an unconditional case of untranslatability'.[17]

In the sadomasochism of 'Anactoria' we find in a series of perfect pairings – reciprocally doublings – this type of poetic suspension: 'lips bruise lips and vein stings vein', fruit 'crushed on fruit' and 'flower on flower':

> My life is bitter with thy love; thine eyes
> Blind me, thy tresses burn me, thy sharp sighs
> Divide my flesh and spirit with soft sound,
> And my blood strengthens, and my veins abound.
> I pray thee sigh not, speak not, draw not breath;
> Let life burn down, and dream it is not death.
> I would the sea had hidden us, the fire
> (Wilt thou fear that, and fear not my desire?)
> Severed the bones that bleach, the flesh that cleaves,
> And let our sifted ashes drop like leaves.
> I feel thy blood against my blood: my pain
> Pains thee, and lips bruise lips, and vein stings vein,
> Let fruit be crushed on fruit, let flower on flower,
> Breast kindle breast, and either burn one hour.

Reviewing Swinburne's *Poems and Ballads* in *The Athenaeum* 4 August 1866, Buchanan charged the poet with producing 'prurient trash and rank blasphemy'.[18] But it was not simply the subject matter to which he objected but also Swinburne's prosody. In discussion of 'Laus Veneris' he writes:

> After a while we find out there is a trick in his very versification, that it owes its music to the most extraordinary style of alliteration [quotes from the poem]. This kind of writing, abounding in adjectives chosen merely because they alliterate, soon cloys and sickens; directly we find out the trick our pleasure departs. We soon perceive that Mr Swinburne's pictures are bright and worthless. We detect no real taste for colour; the skies are all Prussian blue, the flesh tints all vermillion, the sunlights all gamboge.[19]

Just as alliteration is a type of doubling through repetition, the correspondence here between unremitting primary colour and 'fleshly indulgence' intriguingly realizes the extent to which such a correspondence was being made more generally within Pre-Raphaelite works. The physicality of colour, as characterized by Pre-Raphaelite canvases is analogous to the excesses of alliterative poetry; that which Buchanan regards as a surfeit at the linguistic level is best described, he implies, through analogy with Pre-Raphaelite painting.

In a context in which prosody is likened to Pre-Raphaelite canvases the question of whether or not Swinburne may be termed a 'Pre-Raphaelite' poet is a redundant one since, as we see here, from the time of its publication his work is framed by a discourse of Pre-Raphaelitism. Moreover, Buchanan thus reads picture and poem in paired terms but not in those terms in which the poets themselves would have wished to be read. The more radical visual and verbal pairing to which they were committed is here effectively trivialized but it is by no means eclipsed. In another regard, though, Buchanan's charges of subversion were levelled also at a poetic method that jettisoned accepted meaning and made 'sound' as important as 'sense', emptying the signifier of a stable referential value. Furthermore, the 'sound versus sense' argument resembles the image versus text one. For in the manner that he claims image/text relations may hide correspondences, Buchanan considers dangerous, for that which it might occlude, the privileging of sound over sense. What emerges most strongly is that in the ready correspondence between visual and verbal artefacts by definition 'something' threatening is concealed.

Buchanan's review not only damaged the reputations of individual poets but also the project of Pre-Raphaelitism as a whole. In many ways Swinburne's desire to separate poetry from moral responsibility mirrored a radical tendency of Pre-Raphaelitism. Yet, dismissing Swinburne's poems as he did, Buchanan dealt irreparable damage to the already uncertain legacy of the movement. He was also motivated by personal spite because Swinburne's publisher had cancelled a contract with Buchanan for an edition of Keats, instead offering it to Swinburne. In Swinburne's case, Buchanan's attack led to a failure to take his work seriously not only in its heralding of aestheticism but also in its critique of Christianity. Such a critique is especially evident in 'Dolores, Our Lady of Pain', considered by many Swinburne's most sacrilegious poem, in which he constructs a poetic figure whose 'depths of pain and sorrow and her indifference to her worshippers' are 'an affront to the forms of compassion and forgiveness associated with the Virgin Mary'.[20] It is easy to argue that in 'Delores' the 'submission to the overwhelming power of the senses' represents the replacement of one religion by an alternative one but, as Alkalay-Gut points out, 'it is misleading to charge Swinburne with writing simply for the sake of rebelliousness, [...] His work instead analyses the bases of [Victorian] morality and any of his other poems discloses the same kind of complexity'.[21]

Swinburne's interest in forms of complexity is readily apparent in the rhetorical and lexical patterns of his verse but also in the subject matter of his poetry. The figure of the hermaphrodite is especially apt in this regard, representing as it does in the mimetic form of a statue the suspended state of physical and metaphysical doubleness as exemplified by the image/text relation. In the spring of 1863 Swinburne travelled with Whistler to Paris and became fascinated by the Greek statue of the hermaphrodite in the Louvre. Of course the statue 'Hermaphroditus' the Roman copy of a Greek original from the second century BC held a history of fascination; it had previously inspired poems by Percy Shelley and Théophile Gautier.[22] The naked figure is recumbent upon a couch and combines male genitalia with female breasts and bodily contours. Part of the visual enigma it poses is owing to the fact that viewed from one side the statue appears almost uncompromisingly female; while from the other, with the presence of the genitalia, the body marks the incarnation of both sexes in a single human form. Swinburne's poem 'Hermaphroditus' published in *Poems and Ballads* (which recalls Gautier's 'Contralto' from *Emaux et Camées* 1852) realizes the sexually indeterminate body of the hermaphrodite, focusing upon physical perfection as a form of desire frustrated. In part, the poem signals the singular brand of Swinburne's 'Hellenism', and its extreme distinction from that contemporary Hellenistic revival as represented in British poetry for example by Arnold. Moreover, for McGann, Swinburne's reputation as 'a poet of frenzy and incoherence' was significantly owing to the fact that he was 'the most complete of the nineteenth-century hellenes' whose 'revulsion from ordinary Christian standards was recognized and resented'.[23] But in addition, 'Hermaphroditus' unabashedly celebrates 'effeminacy' by promoting a figure of perverse sexuality. By its very title Swinburne's poem plays into the eager hands of Buchanan, confirming his identification of the poet as 'effeminate'. Yet, in its emergence as a type of ekphrastic response to a Greek artefact 'Hermaphroditus' also explores that larger fluctuating relation of painting to poem, of the visual to the auditory sense that we have been exploring. The complex theoretical proposition of the four sonnets was not lost on Swinburne's contemporaries even though it was only really with the Decadent movement that the radicalism of that proposition was fully explored.

The first two lines of Swinburne's poem very interestingly evoke the image of Orpheus and Eurydice, in the gesture of looking back, and one of the enduring attractions of the myth of the tragic lovers resides in representations that present them, as Swinburne does here, as physically bound to one another – androgynous almost:

I

Lift up thy lips, turn round, look back for love,
Blind love that comes by night and casts out rest;

In stanza II the analogy of fire describes the approximate state between sleep and life.

II

Where between sleep and life some brief space is,
    With love like gold bound round about the head,
    Sex to sweet sex with lips and limbs is wed,
Turning the fruitful feud of hers and his
To the waste wedlock of a sterile kiss;
    Yet from them something like as fire is shed
    That shall not be assuaged till death be dead,
Though neither life nor sleep can find out this.

In the third stanza there occurs in the rhetorical question of the
first two lines a series of perfect deferred doublings: 'love/sleep';
'shadow/light' existing in that barely imaginable space between
'eyelids' and 'eyes':

III

Love, is it love or sleep or shadow or light
    That lies between thine eyelids and thine eyes?
Like a flower laid upon a flower it lies,
Or like the night's dew laid upon the night.
Love stands upon thy left hand and thy right,
    Yet by no sunset and by no moonrise
    Shall make thee man and ease a woman's sighs,
Or make thee woman for a man's delight.
To what strange end hath some strange god made fair
    The double blossom of two fruitless flowers?
Hid love in all the folds of all thy hair,
    Fed thee on summers, watered thee with showers,
Given all the gold that all the seasons wear
To thee that art a thing of barren hours?

IV

Yea, love, I see; it is not love but fear.
    Nay, sweet, it is not fear but love, I know;
    Or wherefore should thy body's blossom blow
So sweetly, or thine eyelids leave so clear
Thy gracious eyes that never made a tear –
    Though for their love our tears like blood should flow,
    Though love and life and death should come and go,
So dreadful, so desirable, so dear?
Yea, sweet, I know; I saw in what swift wise
    Beneath the woman's and the water's kiss
    Thy moist limbs melted into Salmacis,
And the large light turned tender in thine eyes,

And all the boy's breath softened into sighs;
But Love being blind, how should he know of this?

In her study *The Female Sublime From Milton to Swinburne: Bearing Blindness* (2001) Catherine Maxwell has explored Swinburne's inclination to the classical forms of catechresis (mixing of metaphors) and chiasmus (contrast by reversing the order).[24] By different means, along with synaesthesia and oxymoron, they allow the poet to heighten the sense of words, draw attention to their materiality, in the creation of suspended states resembling that of the plastic form of hermaphrodite. Indeed, 'contrast and crossing as emblematised in the figure of the hermaphrodite' expose 'a signifying process which is germane to Swinburne's poetics'.[25] 'Hermaphroditus' begins and ends with 'blind love', exploring the relation of the figure of love to that of the emergent hermaphrodite and the phrase 'till death be dead' echoes the earlier form: 'Love, strong as Death, is dead' of Christina Rossetti's 'An End'. A condition of complete and enduring interchangeability characterizes the poem along with barrenness and a structure of desire that eschews procreation, confirming for contemporary critics the extent of Swinburne's sexual 'deviance'. For Thais E. Morgan, for whom 'perversity' forms the main platform of Swinburne's 'aesthetic programme', the 'voyeuristic' perspective of the persona gazing at the statue of the hermaphrodite, as well as the determined 'iconoclasm' of the sonnet sequence overall as an attack on dominant heterosexual mores, place his poem squarely against the majority audience at which Swinburne targets his polemic in the *Notes* : 'the English reader as controlled by "the press" and "the pulpit"'.[26]

UNMANLINESS: SIMEON SOLOMON

The subtext of unmanliness that resonates throughout Buchanan's reviews of Rossetti and Swinburne also echoes, as we've found, throughout criticism of the Pre-Raphaelites. It is similarly present in other reviews of Rossetti's volume such as that in *The Quarterly Review* referring to 'the deification of the animal instincts as emasculate obscenity in *The House of Life*'.[27]

But in Buchanan's review 'unmanliness' is particularly encoded in references to Simeon Solomon's paintings:

> English society of one kind purchases the *Day's Doings*. English society of another kind goes into ecstasy over Mr Solomon's pictures – pretty pictures of morality, such as 'Love dying by the breath of lust'. There is not much to choose between the two objects of admiration except that painters like Mr Solomon lend actual genius to worthless subjects, and therefore produce veritable monsters'.[28]

This is a loaded comment since in 1873 Simeon Solomon artist, writer, and friend of Swinburne would be convicted for indecent exposure and 'attempting to commit sodomy'. In forging such an association with Rossetti, in addition to references to Swinburne, Buchanan barely disguises his homophobic response, one that comes up elsewhere in his writing such as in his critique of Morris' *The Defence of Guenevere*, that is not simply targeted at individual writers and painters but also becomes a response to the wider aesthetic concerns of Pre-Raphaelitism. For Buchanan, Pre-Raphaelite poets and painters epitomize a vague and perverse sensuousness, an excessive preoccupation with issues of form, a lack of regard for the interests of an educated public, and an elevation of the imagination over the intellect.

Solomon is not only a significant painter of the 1860s and 70s, but he also provides a lens through which to focus in the 1870s various general anxieties pertaining to the aesthetic legacy of Pre-Raphaelitism. Indeed, also levelled at Solomon were charges of subversion targeted at the sexual content of Swinburne's verse alongside a persistent fear of homosexuality that haunts Buchanan's critique of the heterosexual love scenarios of Rossetti. It is informative in this regard that following Solomon's arrest for sodomy even so openly controversial a figure as Swinburne failed to write in support of him, and only Walter Pater was willing to stick his neck out in Solomon's defence.[29] Arguably Solomon's most controversial work is the watercolour 'Sacramentum Amoris' of 1868 now lost (possibly destroyed) but which survives in the form of Frederick Hollyer's photographic print. Indeed, photography holds an interesting status in this scenario. While somewhat approximate to call its relationship to the original painting ekphrastic it is the case that the photographic print (not a linguistic 'translation' but a mechanical reproduction of a painting) gives us the original at a remove from it.

'Sacramentum Amoris' is of particular interest for those questions it raises around sexual transgression and the politics of censorship within the doubling function of picture/poem we have so far been tracing. The painting was exhibited at the Fifth General Exhibition of Water-Colour Drawings, Dudley Gallery in 1869 and the theme featured in Solomon's prose poem *A Vision of Love Revealed in Sleep* (1871) 'in which Love appears to the wanderer veiled in a saffron cloak and wearing a fawn-skin: in his hand he carried a staff, which was as the rod of the high priest, for as I looked upon its barrenness burst forth in almond bloom'.[30]

Swinburne reviewed Solomon's prose piece *A Vision of Love Revealed in Sleep* in 1871 in *The Dark Blue*, alluding in particular to the androgynous quality of the figure as one that supersedes the category of sexuality: 'many of [his figures], as the figure bearing the eucharist of love, have a supersexual beauty, in which the lineaments of woman and man seem blended and the lines of sky and landscape melt in burning mist of heat and light'.[31] Swinburne's interpretation of the figure recalls D. G. Rossetti's prototype of the supreme perfection of beauty in man and woman as a point of congruity. By contrast, *The Illustrated London News* objected to Solomon's painting on the grounds of its unwholesome, albeit multiple, signification: 'to perverted fancy the figure with all its symbols may, of course, be made to yield almost any meaning, but scarcely a wholesome or profitable one'.[32] That which Swinburne identifies as the enabling ambivalence of Solomon's androgyne, which in turn recalls D. G. Rossetti's prototype of the perfection of beauty in man and woman, becomes for *The Illustrated London News* the means to an end in a kind of intellectual anarchy.

Without doubt, the commission for the painting was from the start a troubled one for Solomon. His patron, F. R. Leyland, objected to the way in which the male figure was painted and correspondence between Leyland and Solomon reveals the nature of that objection. The artist's intense and eloquent defence of the painting is particularly instructive with regard to the issue of androgyny:

> I mean the whole thing to represent Love in its very highest and most spiritual form, it is therefore sexless; I have mingled the sexes, or endeavoured to do so, in an equal proportion, but I have not made it hermaphrodite in the usual artistic way. The head although not that of a male is not female as you may see by the form of the jaw. Love in it's [sic] highest form is above and beyond consideration of sex, which would at once limit and animalise it, the saffron colored marriage veil covering both the Bridegroom and the Bride mingled in one spiritual form, the Sacrament an outward and visible sign, as the holy things contained in the ark is, like it, covered with cherubim hiding the face. The Thyrsus; like the bush that was burnt but not consumed, has a flame round it and running up it to symbolise that Love which is forever ardent but which can have no end or consummation: the dead stick, blossoming into myrtle flowers, like Aaron's rod that budded, symbolises that what was thought dead is ever freshly blooming; the wings of light to the feet show the spiritual nature of the Love which has little of the earth in it, but, when it touches it, makes flowers spring up at it's [sic] steps; the figure especially the Sacrament, being glowing against a dull background, enjoys the 'Light which showeth in darkness' but that the darkness 'comprehendeth it not' or has no sympathy with it. The Acropolis in ruins at the back, expresses that although the body has passed away the spirit is still living in the figures. The faunskin and girdle have an import of a similar character.[33]

Solomon's admixture of equal proportions of male and female is an attempt to produce a version of spiritual love that is not formally reducible to the figure of the 'hermaphrodite in the usual artistic' sense. He thereby defends his representational choices specifically for their ability to realize spiritual truths without succumbing to the limits of 'animalism'. The detail of his defence dramatizes the difficulties of persuading his patron but also his intense artistic investment in such a symbolic figure. The polite explanation covers Solomon's partial indignation that a viewer may fail to register the spiritual dimension of the image. Emphasis on the significance of the Thyrsus recalls Stephen Bann's reference to Baudelaire 'whose cultivation of "synaesthesia" reinvigorated the classical tradition of *ekphrasis*, introducing a wide variety of sensory associations in order to parallel the sensuous abundance of paint'.[34] As we shall find, Solomon's defence and the explanation of the personification of the figure of 'Love' in the poem closely resemble Rossetti's defence of Dante's depiction of the same figure in his translation of *La Vita Nuova*. For both emphasize the sensuous physical embodiment of a spiritual state.

6

Rossetti's reading of Dante's
La Vita Nuova

Rossetti began translating *La Vita Nuova* in 1846, just prior to the establishment of the Pre-Raphaelite brotherhood, and first published it together with *The Early Italian Poets* in 1861; he republished it in 1874 as *Dante and his Circle*. Dante's 'Autopsychology' as Rossetti called it, that fascinated him throughout his life, takes the form of autobiographical prose narrative interlaced with sonnets. Rossetti's translation of the *Vita Nuova* is a crucial text in understanding the significance to the Pre-Raphaelite cause of the figures of 'Love' and of 'Beatrice'. There are many reasons why the Dante/Beatrice relationship would appeal to Rossetti and to other Pre-Raphaelite painters and poets; a key one is the notion of the artist's soul embodied in the female form; another is that Dante's sonnets, and his commentaries upon them, privilege 'Love' personified as a male figure in ways that invite visual representation. The sonnets subsequently enable the emergence of particular figures of sexual ambivalence as depicted in the work of Swinburne and Solomon. Moreover, the relationship of Dante and Beatrice resonates throughout Pre-Raphaelitism, not simply in the obvious sense of a poetic and artistic model of medieval idealized love (which it certainly was), but also as a relationship of excessive emotion twinned with a disproportionate amount of bodily contact or fulfilment. The *Vita Nuova* is also fundamental to this study for those ways in which Dante's representation of vision, and Rossetti's translator's gloss upon it, sheds light upon the power of sight as a principle metaphor for the Pre-Raphaelites. Dante's text is about realizing intangible things and, most specifically for our purposes, of rendering visible the image/text relation and realizing the physicality of language.

Early in his translation of the *Vita Nuova* Rossetti marks himself out as a reader of Dante who prefers to court, rather than resolve, ambiguity in his translation. Thus, on the issue of the meaning of the 'new' of the title, its signification of 'young' as well as 'new', Rossetti prefers, in contrast to some editors, what he terms 'the more mystical interpretation of the words', 'as New Life' over 'Early Life'.[1] This formula also comes some way to explaining Dante's wider use of personification in the *Vita Nuova* a method that, as Rossetti explains, is crucial to its meaning. Dante outlines in elaborate detail his reasons for ascribing to 'Love', 'Death' and 'Sorrow' physical embodiment. On the personification of love he writes:

> It might be here objected unto me, [...] that I have spoken of Love as though it were a thing outward and visible: not only a spiritual essence, but as a bodily substance also. The which thing, in absolute truth, is a fallacy; Love not being of itself a substance, but an accident of substance. Yet that I speak of Love as though it were a thing tangible and even human, appears by three things which I say thereof. And firstly, I say that I perceived Love coming towards me [...] And secondly, I say that Love smiled; and thirdly, that Love spake. (VN 107–9)

Fundamentally, Dante constructs 'Love' as an overpowering male presence; there is a homoerotic element to the triangular relationship of speaker, beloved, and the figure of 'Love' as male, which is compromised or squared by the further function of the 'screen' lover. Moreover, the figure of 'Love' corresponds somewhat with that of the hermaphrodite as we've discussed it in Swinburne and Solomon. There is a strong desire on the part of Dante's speaker to surrender to the embodied presence of 'Love'. The subject of the first sonnet, which recalls Dante's first vision of Beatrice, reflecting his joy following his receipt of her salutation, is apt in this respect. 'Love' comes to Dante as 'a lordly figure, frightening to behold, yet in himself [...] he was filled with a marvellous joy' (*VN* 107). Throughout the sequence Dante articulates his actions as his 'obedience to Love's will':

> In his arms it seemed to me that a person was sleeping, covered only with a blood coloured cloth; upon whom looking very attentively, I knew that it was the lady of the salutation who had deigned the day before to salute me. And

he who held her held also in his hand a thing that was burning in flames; and he said to me, Vide cor tuum ['Behold thy heart']. But when he had remained with me a little while, I thought that he set himself to awaken her that slept; after the which he made her to eat that thing which flamed in his hand; and she ate as one fearing. (VN 80–81)

In Dante's vivid dream we encounter a graphic embodiment of corporeal as spiritual love. Significantly, Rossetti translates the 'cloth' that covers Beatrice as 'blood coloured' and not 'crimson' as do other translators of Dante, for he holds the colour closer to the corporeal. The eating of the heart, having both divine and sadomasochistic resonance, stresses the crucial status of the vision/dream in staging desire for Rossetti as well as Dante.

Yet in the *Vita Nuova* the eyes come before the mouth of the beloved. Of course eyes figure prominently in the conceits of Petrarchan sonnet sequences; it was customary to itemize the beloved's physical attributes such that eyes often gained prominence as the apertures to the soul and, in their mirroring function, as the locus of reflection of the speaker himself. Early on in the text Dante writes:

I admit that among the words in which I set forth the occasion of the sonnet there are some whose meaning is obscure, for instance when I say that Love slays all my spirits, except the spirits of vision, which survive but are driven forth from their organs. It is impossible to explain this to anyone who is not to some extent a faithful follower of Love; and to those who are it is obvious what the meaning is. (VN 93)

Dante ponders why, physically disfigured by his pain at seeing Beatrice, he should long to 'behold her', to which a 'humble thought said in reply': 'If I were master of all my faculties [...] I would tell her that no sooner do I imagine to myself her marvellous beauty that I am possessed with the desire to behold her, the which is of so great strength that it kills and destroys in my memory all the things which might oppose it' (*VN* 93). Moreover, in Dante's desire for Beatrice the direct gaze is, for the large part, mediated by the 'screen' lover whom he adopts to disguise his interest: 'and betwixt her and me, in a direct line, there sat another lady of pleasant favour [...] marvelling at my continued gaze which seemed to have her for its subject' (*VN* 93).

The figure of the 'screen' in Dante's text, as a method of

diverting attention from the real object of his gaze and affection, is fascinating not least because in order to appear plausible the 'screen' must generate her own discourse in the form of sonnets (*VN* 82–3). In this sense, not only does the function of the 'screen' love seem more than accidentally appropriate to a nineteenth century context, in its meaning of obscuring or absorbing in order to protect that which lies beyond it, the noun 'screen' also introduces a topical optical sense as a surface upon which things are projected. Furthermore, throughout the text, as well as generating poetry, Dante's act of gazing at the beloved is inseparable from a desire to gain her verbal greeting. Thus the eyes and the mouth sustain a vital correspondence in the *Vita Nuova* such that the eyes *'are the beginning of love'* while *'the mouth,*[...] *is the end of love'*. Dante continues:

> that every vicious thought may be discarded herefrom, let the reader remember that it is above written that the greeting of this lady, which was an act of her mouth, was the goal of my desires, while I could receive it (*VN* 99).

The place of the mouth here is especially crucial as the generator of the word. Language is realized most overtly by the primacy of the mouth in the text. It is a synecdoche for speech, salutation, as well as sexual ingress. Dante substitutes the mouth (as the end of love) in sexual terms, for the mouth as the seat of salutation such that a balance occurs. Beatrice's denial to Dante of her salutation is reciprocally a denial of her kiss. Speech and kisses come together for Rossetti in ways that trope the larger sister arts analogy: the poem the utterance; the painting the kiss. It is Beatrice's salutation that Dante craves and the absence of her salutation that so deeply affects him. The mouth here, then, is not so much the locus of kisses, as in Rossetti's already kissed mouth of the the painting *Bocca Baciata*, but instead the locus of language, of speech: not the extravagant speech of love but of greeting 'was the goal of [his] desires'. In larger theoretical terms, the *Vita Nuova* encapsulates for Rossetti the absence of dichotomy he strives for in the body/soul relationship. There is no distinction between the bodily and the spiritual, for the spiritual marks the body as in the deep coloured rings that appear around his eyes following Dante's uncontrollable weeping. Thus, somewhat indirectly via Rossetti's very personal investment in Dante's *La Vita Nuova*, we both anticipate, and are led back to the word as flesh, and to the significance of Rossetti's manuscript book with which we began: the book as corporeal.

In this context, Dante's imagined death of Beatrice is key to the text not least owing to those possibilities it offers to focus resurrection. Dante's 'vision' of Beatrice was he claims 'so strong' that 'it made [him] to behold my lady in death; whose head certain ladies seemed to be covering with a white veil' (*VN* 104). Following Dante's example, the painting *Dante's dream of the death of Beatrice* recurs hauntingly in Rossetti's later years. He first made a small watercolour of the subject for Ellen Heaton in 1856 but in 1869 he was commissioned by William Graham to produce an oil version. Although Rossetti finished the painting in 1871, Graham rejected it for being too large; Rossetti finally sold it to the City of Liverpool in 1881. The painting shows the corpse of Beatrice laid out upon a bier, attended by two female figures. The figure of Dante is led by the hand of the figure of 'Love' who leans over to kiss Beatrice and, as Rossetti explains in his ekphrasis to the painting, 'As he reaches the bier, Love bends for a moment over Beatrice with the kiss which her lover has never given her, while the two dream-ladies hold the pall of may bloom suspended for an instant before it covers her face for ever'.[2] In Dante's dream 'Love' mediates between himself and his beloved. The longed for kiss belongs to 'Love' here and the homoeroticism generated by the physical embodiment of 'Love' in the *Vita Nuova* is perhaps more directly conveyed in the painting where the proximity of the male figures, their joined hands and Dante's submissive relation to 'Love', signals a unity enduring or superseding that of desire for an individual beloved.

During the latter part of his life, like Dante's duplicate loved 'image' the screen that retains the secret of his gaze, Rossetti manipulated his relationship to the beloved in the various depictions of the death of Beatrice. In an extract from his diary of 30 May 1877 W. M. Rossetti's writes: 'A letter from Gabriel to Mamma shows that he is now occupied on the smaller replica of his "Death of Beatrice" picture'. On 5 August 1878, '[Rossetti] is ... somewhat advanced with the smaller duplicate of his "Death of Beatrice"', and in June 1881 '[he] has begun making, in his large picture of "The Death of Beatrice" a certain change in the drapery [...] to correspond with the smaller picture'.[3]

Rossetti duplicates replicas and he paints 'Dante drawing an angel on the anniversary of the first death of Beatrice' as an oscillation of light and shadow that sustains the dilemma of vision and desire. In all these examples, painting and mourning come together as forms of compulsive repetition via the symbolic figure of Beatrice. It is not surprising that Rossetti could not finish the paintings, that they generated replicas. For the act of painting, as here realized, only briefly satisfies a compulsion to repeat the figure – returning us to a desire to take in the face of a beloved. Since it occupies the status of a compulsion the gesture must be repeated. But, as we shall find, it is the face of the beloved in death, or envisioned in death, that above all demands to be repeatedly represented.

7

The Shade

It is perhaps not surprising given the melancholic history we've glimpsed that D. G. Rossetti's work is peopled by many embodiments of the shade. Both paintings and poems are haunted by personae that inhabit unearthly realms. Those female figures we have previously encountered remain throughout his work but acquire a degree of persistence in the later period. *Beata Beatrix* (1864) is an important painting for crystallizing various strands of Rossetti's aesthetic and for impressing the means by which in Pre-Raphaelitism more generally the literary, artistic and the personal become thoroughly entwined. A painting that tends to be thought of chiefly as a portrait of Elizabeth Siddal, a tribute after her death, was conceived as a painting about Dante, Beatrice and the figure of Love, as we've seen so central to the *Vita Nuova*. In its completed state the ecstatic figure of Beatrice receiving the poppy dominates the composition spatially. But, in terms of colouring, the background figures of Dante, and Love, prominent in red, who holds out the flaming heart, are given equal weight and they haunt the portrait format together with the unmistakable Florentine outline of the Ponte Vecchio which bridges the Arno.

Although at one level *Beata Beatrix* is clearly a portrait of Siddal, it is important to locate the painting within the complex process of Rossetti's identification with Dante. In many ways, following Dante, Rossetti's incarnation of 'Love' himself, and his almost masochistic enslavement to that figure, holds more of a sway over his work than any individual person. In such a reading it is the power of identification, Rossetti's compulsion to identify with particular masochistic figures, that is particularly telling. Indeed, to all intents and purposes, as I've suggested, that compulsion renders as approximate self-portraits Rossetti's

100

portraits of women. Moreover, a wish to inhabit, both in thought and in a visual context, a space between life and death as one brought about by extreme desire, is perhaps most uncompromisingly explored by Rossetti in the figure of Proserpine.

PROSERPINE

A pervasive desire for the interchangeability of art forms is indeed a driving force of later works by Swinburne, Solomon and Watts. The fascination for, or insistence upon, re-imagining a theme or a figure such as Proserpine is crucial, emerging as it does from a Pre-Raphaelite aesthetic articulated early on in *The Germ*. Rossetti began the painting *Proserpine* (Plate 3), modelled on Jane Morris, in 1874. The relatively late conception of the painting testifies to the extent to which, in spite of his illness, Rossetti was still able to produce some of his very best work. Not only does the theme of the resurrected woman remain, however, it also gains impetus. Proserpine, daughter of the goddess Ceres, is literally dead to the world for six months of each year while she resides in Hades with Pluto. Her subterranean existence was the result of her having tasted seven grains of the pomegranate, fruit of the underworld. Rossetti depicts Proserpine in a space lit only by a patch of light that illuminates the wall, her face and figure. An incense burner, attribute of the goddess, appears in the foreground and ivy arches in the background emerging from behind the attached sonnet written into the painting in Italian as if appended to the wall:

Afar away the light that brings cold cheer
Unto this wall, – one instant and no more
Admitted at my distant palace-door.
Afar the flowers of Enna from this drear
Dire fruit, which, tasted once, must thrall me here.
Afar those skies from this Tartarean grey
That chills me; and afar, how far away,
The nights that shall be from the days that were.

Afar from mine own self I seem, and wing
Strange ways in thought, and listen for a sign:
And still some heart unto some soul doth pine,

3 Dante Gabriel Rossetti, *Proserpine* (1874) Tate Britain

(Whose sounds mine inner sense is fain to bring,
Continually together murmuring,) –
'Woe's me for thee, unhappy Proserpine!'

Rossetti was fascinated by the fate of Proserpine and produced eight oil versions of which only four have survived and one of which he was attempting to complete in the days leading up to his death. Critics praised 'the Symbolist power' of the painting and, owing to its 'iconic quality', many regarded it as Rossetti's greatest work (Marsh 460). *Proserpine* is a highly evocative image not least owing to the way it conflates the fleetingness of a moment, as symbolized by the physical patch of light, with the eternal despair of the figure. Combining iconicity with transience, the world of light fractures the darkness by way of its projection onto the wall. In a letter of 10 August 1875 to Frederick Stephens Rossetti tells the story of the origin of that patch of light:

> she is passing along a gloomy corridor of her palace, and a sharp light (as if an upper door opening suddenly flashed down for a moment the light of the outer world) strikes on the wall behind her, throwing her head and massive hair into strong relief, as she turns her eyes sadly towards the distinct gleam. (DW)

The iconic figure is thus shown at a particular temporal moment as signalled by the 'flash' of light. The relative awkwardness of the hands, displaying the red gash of the fruit, and the torsion of the figure contribute to a sensuousness of the surface that is broken by the sonnet. It is the paring down of the composition that is so distinctive here, together with the overt melancholy of the subject.

Yet, within the identifiably symbolist contours of *Proserpine*, there exists a link back to that Ruskinian botanizing discussed earlier. While Rossetti's artistic uses of fruit and flowers are far different from Ruskin's, there is a connection in their high degree of naturalism as invested with intense emotion and personally encoded symbolism. The curving ivy branch forms, for Rossetti, 'along with the swaying lines of the drapery the pictorial motive of the design' (DW) a kind of anchor in the empirical world; that which we have found to be at one level a prop for the troubled psyche. Within the composition of *Proserpine* the doubling sonnet is contained, pinned to the trellis. As previously encountered, the pervasive desire for the inter-changeability of painting and poem resonates in Rossetti's initially imagined and re-imagined 'double' work. The sonnet 'Proserpina' for the picture is spoken by Proserpine herself but incorporates, in the final line, her self-consciousness of the reflection of another upon her fate: 'Woe's me for thee, unhappy Proserpine!'

The shift in perspective in 'Proserpina' echoes the oscillation between first and third person perspective characteristic of Tennyson's lyrics. But whereas Armstrong has shown the 'double' poem works for poets such as Tennyson and Browning within a single text, Rossetti employs a doubling facility in the interplay between poem and painting. However, the project of conjoining visual and verbal assumes a different inflection here where the materiality of the poem is impressed upon the eye by way of its *trompe l'oeil* status as a kind of cartouche within the frame. Rossetti's signature appears similarly appended with *trompe l'oeil* effect at the bottom of the painting. Integral to the image is a Blakeian scenario of painted words: there to be read but, first and foremost, to be seen. Again we find here a subtle ekphrastic relationship distinctly configured in a work that contains painted words as integral to the composition. Swinburne was himself drawn to the myth of Proserpine. His 'Garden of Proserpine' and 'Hymn to Proserpine' both appeared in *Poems and Ballads* (1866). [2] Stanza VII of 'The Garden of Proserpine' conjures for us in advance a version of Rossetti's iconic figure:

> Pale, beyond porch and portal,
> Crowned with calm leaves, she stands
> Who gathers all things mortal
> With cold immortal hands.
> Her languid lips are sweeter
> Than love's who fears to greet her
> To men that mix and meet her
> From many times and lands.

EURYDICE

The story of Proserpine is prescient for it leads albeit indirectly

to that of Eurydice. The two tales are connected not only by
their underworld setting (Proserpine is Pluto's wife and
Orpheus' song moves Pluto and Proserpine to allow him to
take back Eurydice) but also by the act of seeing itself, by those
ways in which seeing is figured principally in each tale as a
desire for a returned look. It is Orpheus' fateful decision to
transgress the prohibition on looking back, his gaze at Eurydice,
which results in his losing her a second time. In Rossetti's
painting and poem, Proserpine's fate, her half yearly incarcera-
tion in the underworld, is figured in terms of vision, the
reflected patch of light as key to that which is denied the 'life' of
a shade.

Rossetti refers to the figure of Orpheus in Sonnet V1 of *The
House of Life*, entitled 'The Kiss':

> What smouldering senses in death's sick delay
>> Or seizure of malign vicissitude
>> Can rob this body of honour, or denude
> This soul of wedding-raiment worn to-day?
> For lo! even now my lady's lips did play
>> With these my lips such consonant interlude
>> As laurelled Orpheus longed for when he wooed
> The half-drawn hungering face with that last lay.
>
> I was a child beneath her touch, – a man
>> When breast to breast we clung, even I and she, –
>> A spirit when her spirit looked through me, –
> A god when all our life-breath met to fan
> Our life-blood, till love's emulous ardours ran,
>> Fire within fire, desire in deity.

Thus death has a voice in *The House of Life*, for the 'consonant
interlude' for which Orpheus longs is that with Eurydice. She is
thereby present in the sonnet analogously: the 'half-drawn
hungry face' a spectre of loss. Moreover, it is as if for Rossetti the
mythological figure of Proserpine operates at one remove from
Eurydice and may thereby hold, without signalling too overtly,
the significance of Orpheus' failure to obey the injunction to
'look back'. Given such an associative relation between the
figures of Eurydice and Proserpine, Rossetti toiled over the latter
as an approximate and less distressing figure for Eurydice. Thus,
there exists a further use of doubling here as a type of defence
mechanism: the mythological figure of Proserpine haunts

4 Frederic Leighton, *Orpheus and Eurydice* (1864)
Leighton House Museum

Rossetti's work indirectly as shade or spectre. While Rossetti realizes Proserpine visually, he does so in part because Eurydice offers too painful and perfect a congruence between that mythological figure and his own lost love. In a sense Proserpine works for Rossetti rather like the 'screen' lover does for Dante in the *Vita Nuova*, a figure with which, as we have found, he was extremely familiar through his translation of that text. Nevertheless, there are striking differences between Orpheus' and Rossetti's compulsion to communicate with a shade. There is heroism implicit in Orpheus' desire to rescue Eurydice that does not accompany Rossetti's wish to retrieve his buried poems. Although Rossetti couched his act in a desire for art, at some level such reasoning remained for him unconvincing.

In the power of its longing, Robert Browning's lyric from *Dramatis Personae*, 'Eurydice to Orpheus' subtitled 'A Picture by Leighton', written to accompany Frederic Leighton's painting *Orpheus and Eurydice* (Plate 4) exhibited at the Royal Academy in 1864, might well serve as an influence upon Rossetti:

> But give them me, the mouth, the eyes, the brow!
> Let them once more absorb me! One look now
>   Will lap me round for ever, not to pass
> Out of its light, though darkness lie beyond:
> Hold me but safe again within the bond
>   Of one immortal look! All woe that was,
> Forgotten, and all terror that may be,
> Defied, – no past is mine, no future: look at me!

Here Eurydice's invocation to Orpheus to give to her 'one immortal look' encapsulates that condition of temporal suspension, or arrest, that Blanchot, writing in his seminal essay 'The Gaze of Orpheus', conceptualizes as 'this one concern: to look into the night at what the night is concealing – the *other* night, concealment which becomes invisible' (Blanchot 100). For Blanchot the myth shows that Orpheus' destiny:

> does not demand Eurydice in her diurnal truth and her everyday charm, but in her nocturnal darkness, in her distance, her body closed, her face sealed, which wants to see her not when she is visible but when she is invisible, and not as the intimacy of a familiar life, but as the strangeness of that which excludes all intimacy; it does not want to make her live, but to have the fullness of her death living in her. (Blanchot 99–100)

The desire is to see the 'invisible': for Blanchot the plenitude of death living in the body of the beloved. Blanchot's gloss on Orpheus' desire might well describe Rossetti's relationship to the image of Siddal which, in the manner of Dante's relation to Beatrice, represents a demand for her 'in her nocturnal darkness, in her distance, her body closed, [...] to have the fullness of her death living in her'. Such a desire is implicit in those images of Eurydice, of Francesca de Rimini, of Rossetti's many versions of Proserpine and Beatrice. These images do not represent 'the dead woman' so much in Bronfen's sense of the term as one in which the power of the look is fundamental and what is looked *at* is a form of 'strangeness' to which resurrection is key.

Browning's dramatic persona, the shade Eurydice and her desire to receive the 'look', opens up the other side of what it is about the myth that preoccupied nineteenth-century poets and painters. The tale has been read frequently from the position of Orpheus and his art, the song, whose power is such that it moves all who hear it, reducing Pluto to iron tears. In this sense, the myth functions as a parable of an artist and his muse in which Eurydice has no agency in relation to her fate. Browning, by contrast, pondering Leighton's painting, releases a voice from within what becomes for Blanchot the 'sealed' face of Eurydice. The visual medium of painting generates a space in which to articulate a female voice.[3] Furthermore, the fact that Browning articulates Eurydice's desire for 'the look' opens up that other side of looking thus overturning more common conceptions of the dead woman as object of the male look.

In addition to his *Orpheus and Eurydice* (1864) Leighton painted an earlier composition *The Triumph of Music: Orpheus by the Power of his Art redeems his Wife from Hades*[4] in 1856 (present whereabouts unknown) that evokes an important ekphrastic relationship in those interconnected artefacts that hold the Orpheus/Eurydice myth at their core. In the relationship of visual to verbal as played out in the association of Browning's poem with Leighton's now lost painting – a state of equipoise that allows to emerge here the voice of the usually silenced Eurydice – Browning takes up what is in Leighton's interpretation an unusual reading of the myth. Browning dramatizes the woman's desire and Orpheus' reluctance to look: his averted

5 George Frederic Watts, *Orpheus and Eurydice* (1869)
Aberdeen Art Gallery and Museums Collection

eyes. Eurydice is the instigator of the look here. An ekphrastic relationship between visual and verbal surfaces such that Browning's pondering of Leighton's picture releases a voice from within what is for Blanchot the 'sealed' face of Eurydice. That voice, the voice of the shade, is clear and imploring: 'but give them me, the mouth, the eyes, the brow' – in its desire is to be absorbed in Orpheus' look, to be held captive in his act of looking upon her in death. Eurydice's desire for Orpheus' 'look' exceeds thus the tragic weight of its consequences. In the poetic moment of utterance the desire for the look supersedes all sense of time. In Browning's version the look represents for Eurydice perpetual light in darkness.

George Frederic Watts' remarkable painting *Orpheus and Eurydice* (1869–72) (Plate 5)[5] highlights Rossetti's drive to embody a subtle yet compulsive fascination with figures of resurrection. Watts takes up the injunction to Orpheus not to look back, showing us the moment of Orpheus' refusal to disavow the return of the look: that form of specularity which results in Eurydice's dying a second time. Rather in the manner of Rossetti's relationship with the figure of Proserpine, Watts returned to the myth of Orpheus and Eurydice again and again in his painting from the 1860s onwards, exhibiting one version at the Royal Academy Summer Exhibition in 1867. He was fascinated by the attempt to depict the moment of loss, producing smaller works in preparation for a large picture. The large version, exhibited to great acclaim at the Grosvenor Gallery in 1879, most strikingly realizes the outcome of that 'fateful' look; Eurydice's pale lifeless body falls away from that of Orpheus as he tries to support her still with his arm.[6] The iconic quality of the work marks out the later evolution of the aesthetic of Pre-Raphaelitism in a form similar to that found in Solomon's work.

Jay Prosser in *Light in the Dark Room Photography and Loss* has taken up Roland Barthes' relationship to the Orpheus myth as it relates to his exploration of the palinode as a figure for photography.[7] Reading Barthes' *Camera Lucida* as a work not of mourning but of melancholia, a realization of his inability to move forward following the death of his mother, Prosser charts the reappearance of the myth throughout Barthes' writing career. In *Camera Lucida* it is the photographer's 'second sight' which consists not in 'seeing' but in giving the sense to the photograph of pure accidental presence, the detail (the punctum) that will gaze back at Barthes: 'above all, imitating Orpheus, he must not turn back to look at what he is leading – what he is giving to me!' (Barthes cited in Prosser 36):

> In *Camera Lucida* Barthes *enacts* the Orpheus myth, because he *does* look back, finally, fatally, fails the injunction to look forward, to progress. Orpheus is, of course, a myth about melancholia – about unsuccessful, refused mourning.

But as Prosser asks:

> why look back – a question that surely is what fascinates about the myth – if not in order to look upon death itself, or because the love is so extreme it overrides the injunction, can't abide the gods' law? (Prosser 37)

These conditions of 'melancholia' and 'unsuccessful mourning' as realized in the Orpheus and Eurydice myth that Prosser draws out of *Camera Lucida* hold a powerful resonance for Rossetti, and the figure of Proserpine serves as a potentially redeemed emblem for it. Rossetti is Orpheus-like in his journey to retrieve his poems from the subterranean world; there is a type of equivalence to the myth enacted in the episode of recovering the poems but it is a highly modified one. Equally, Rossetti may be said to violate the Orpheus principle. Whereas the power of Orpheus' song moved the gods to allow him to enter the underworld, Rossetti forces his way into the grave to take back the 'song' he had originally bestowed as tribute to his beloved. Nevertheless, Rossetti's song must be recovered from the underworld at great expense just as in going to Hades Orpheus must lose Eurydice a second time.

Although Rossetti only openly identifies with Orpheus on one occasion, the aforementioned sonnet, the injunction not to look back, not to open Siddal's grave, haunts him both before and after his act of opening it. He produced a little known pencil drawing 'Orpheus and Eurydice' in 1875[8] that shows Orpheus leading Eurydice out of Hades, over the Styx at the moment of looking back. Proserpine appears a lamenting figure enthroned behind them with Pluto who draws back a curtain to reveal a stairway leading up to earth. A grotesque sphinx figure cowering on the staircase emphasizes the overall sense of foreboding. Significantly, Rossetti chooses to depict that scene of the fateful look back to the face of Eurydice.

Swinburne's second volume *Songs Before Sunrise* (1871), by contrast, includes a poem entitled 'Eurydice' (to Victor Hugo) that fuses different temporal episodes of the tale:

> Orpheus, the night is full of tears and cries,
>> And hardly for the storm and ruin shed
>> Can even thine eyes be certain of her head
> Who never passed out of thy spirit's eyes,
> But stood and shone before them in such wise
>> As when with love her lips and hands were fed,
>> And with mute mouth out of the dusty dead
> Strove to make answer when thou bad'st her rise.
>
> Yet viper-stricken must her lifeblood feel
>> The fang that stung her sleeping, the foul germ
>> Even when she wakes of hell's most poisonous worm,
> Though now it writhe beneath her wounded heel.
>> Turn yet, she will not fade nor fly from thee;
>> Wait, and see hell yield up, Eurydice.

The sonnet shifts from the present context of Hades through the more distant past of Orpheus' love of Eurydice to her fatal wounding by a viper. Its invocation is to Orpheus and there remains optimism in the trajectory of the verse in which what becomes a fatal act of looking back falls beyond the frame of the poem. Swinburne focuses upon the assured prospect of the final couplet, the moment at which hell will 'yield up, Eurydice' in spite of his 'turn[ing]'. The first stanza conveys the chaos of hell's landscape, of Orpheus' impossible task to distinguish among the shades of Hades, which Virgil in the *Georgics* so powerfully likens to 'millions of birds that hide in the leaves/ When evening or winter rain from the hills has driven them'. The second stanza articulates her internal state as altered by the viper's poison. Rather than an injunction *not* to look, or a meditation upon the punishment for looking, the poem advocates with controlled assurance, defiance almost, the act of looking: 'turn yet, she will not fade nor fly from thee'.

Swinburne's poem perhaps owes more to Virgil's account of Orpheus and Eurydice in the *Georgics* rather than to Ovid's better known version in the *Metamorphoses* (4. 453-527). Virgil writes:

112

But, by his song aroused from Hell's nethermost basements,
Flocked out the flimsy shades, the phantoms lost to light,
In number like to the millions of birds that hide in the leaves
When evening or winter rain from the hills has driven them –
Mothers and men, the dead
Bodies of great-heart heroes, boys and unmarried maidens,
Young men laid on the pyre before their parents' eyes –
And about them lay the black ooze, the crooked reeds of
     Cocytus,
Bleak the marsh that barred them in with stagnant water,
And the Styx coiling nine times around corralled them there.
Why, Death's very home and holy of holies was shaken
To hear that song, and the Furies with steel-blue snakes
     Entwined
In their tresses; the watch-dog Cerberus gaped open his
     Triple mouth;
Ixion's wheel stopped dead from whirling in the wind
And now he's avoided every pitfall of the homeward path,
Close behind him (for this condition has Proserpine made),
When a moment's madness catches her lover off his guard –
Pardonable, you'd say, but Death can never pardon.
He Halts. Eurydice, his own, as now on the lip of
Daylight. Alas! He forgot. His purpose broke. He looked back.
His labour was lost, the pact he had made with the merciless
     King
Annulled. Three times did thunder peel over the pools of
     Avernus.
'Who,' she cried, 'has doomed me to misery, who has
     Doomed us?
What madness beyond measure? Once more a cruel fate
Drags me away, and my stormy eyes are drowned in
     Darkness.
Good-bye. I am bourne away. A limitless night is about me
And over the strengthless hands I stretch to you, yours no
     Longer.'
Thus she spoke: and at once from his sight, like a wisp of
     Smoke
Thinned into air, was gone.[9]

One of the most interesting details of Virgil's version of the myth is the way in which Orpheus' desire to look round occurs precisely at that point at which Eurydice becomes visible as she 'verges' upon the light, as if the point at which she becomes newly perceptible incites a desire to see her. In addition, Virgil gives Eurydice a voice, though one very different from Browning's, by which to articulate her desire for 'the look'. Virgil's Eurydice utters words of tragic resignation while somewhat unexpectedly, perhaps, Swinburne offers as an affirmative version of the tale's ending, one that, by way of a kind of dare almost, defies eternal separation and sustains hope of reunion.

Both Watts' and Rossetti's decisions to paint from classical myth reinforce the attraction to the artists of *ut pictura poesis*. Furthermore, the insistent place of resurrection that emerges most powerfully in these examples of Beatrice, Proserpine and Eurydice is key to the Pre-Raphaelite aesthetic that aspires to a slippage between image and text, painting and poem. A late canvas by Watts entitled *Love and Death* (1885–7) is significant in this regard, as one in which the artist claimed to have aspired to a 'new' category of art, that he later called 'poems painted on canvas'.[10] Indeed, in a letter to Charles Rickards of 27 December 1884, Watts glosses his method in the painting he continually reworked until 1887 as a desire to '[prove] that Art, like Poetry and Music may suggest the noblest and tenderest thoughts, inspiring and awakening, if only for a time, the highest sensibilities of our nature.'[11]

The slippage between media that Watts aspires to in 'poems painted on canvas' re-works the sister-arts analogy that, as we have found, forms a kernel of Pre-Raphaelitism. The Pre-Raphaelites radically rewrite the doctrine of *ut pictura poesis* such that it becomes not only a simple interrelationship between image and text in an aesthetic of mimesis but it also performs other versions and conditions of that relationship. Watts' above example is especially resonant since 'poems painted on canvas' would appear to be a far cry from Pre-Raphaelite principles. At one level, we see gestures towards Watts' ideal in those visual allusions to music: the incorporations of musical instruments in Rossetti's work. The figure of Orpheus is inseparable from his lyre, and it is his song that allows him into Hades, to 'look' at death. Watts depicts his figure of Orpheus famously with his instrument. Although one might make a simple correspondence between Pater's aesthetic theory and Pre-Raphaelitism by way of the representation of musical instruments – all art famously 'aspiring to the condition of music' – there is a larger correspondence to be made in terms of the musicality of Swinburne's verse.

Yet, Watts' wish to paint the linguistic, to give language a visual resonance in the manner of pigment, is far different from wanting to incorporate visual imagery into a poem. He aspires to the artistry of a poet and, in so doing, he is not simply aspiring to what he regards as the sovereign status of the poet but rather he is setting out to achieve a condition in painting that he believes belongs to poetry but may be imported from it. Watts' gloss on *Love and Death* thus transports us back to the enduring fascination of the sister arts analogy: its apparent promise of something inimitable to emerge from the mutual transaction between the two; resurrection endures as a powerful metaphor for this possibility.

As we have discovered, this type of movement, whereby an additional voice or register is revealed in the correspondence between visual and verbal, between painting and poem, is one of the chief attractions for the Pre-Raphaelites of the aesthetic of *ut pictura poesis*. Often it occurs in the space between poem and painting but at other times it surfaces from within a discrete poem, as in Swinburne's work in which particular visual details aspire to hallucinatory effect. For example the dwelling upon a physical presence or mark, most famously the fleck of blood in 'Laus Veneris', registers a disruption of an accepted relationship between the visual and verbal: 'For her neck,/ Kissed over close, wears yet a purple speck/Wherein the pained blood falters and goes out;/ Soft, and stung softly – fairer for a fleck' (*Poems and Ballads*). Such concentration produces instability within language that is reciprocally a kind of precariousness in the visual field. Swinburne opens up a space within poetic language where the visual becomes newly insistent. In the critical alarm caused by what was regarded as the deceitfulness of Swinburne's consummate prosody, its ability to hide immorality in its mellifluousness, we encounter a response to a different type of visual and verbal balancing. As we have found, such recourse to a form of *ut pictura poesis* has a fundamental function in Pre-Raphaelite works. If we consider again the hallucinatory quality of Pre-Raphaelite canvases, on the surface they appear far from the works of Swinburne, Watts and Solomon. However, a connection emerges in that space between visual and verbal as articulated through an ekphrastic relationship conjuring the possibility of a speaking picture and a mute poem.

Afterthought

The figure of resurrection returns us to that context of Rossetti's exhumation of his verse with which we began. And I want to end by going back now to the place in this study of the disinterment of Rossetti's little book, to dwell finally upon the power it has had to fundamentally inflect discourses of Pre-Raphaelitism. Indeed, I want to claim that, aside from its actual physical occurrence, even if Rossetti hadn't exhumed the book, a thought (if not an act) of exhumation, reciprocally of resurrection, would still haunt the movement. For, resurrection encapsulates the fundamental dilemma of transformation within image/text relations that preoccupied the Pre-Raphaelites. Such a quality of return is present, as I hope to have demonstrated, in those repeated preoccupations with resurrected figures, with a death that is not final; in Christina Rossetti's voices from the grave; in the lost and resurrected forms of Ophelia and Chatterton, of Beatrice, of Proserpine, of Eurydice to name but a few.

Yet somewhat remarkably we also already find the motif of exhumation writ large in a curious occasion of second sight in D. G. Rossetti's poem from 1848 originally titled in manuscript 'Unburied Death'.[1] When publishing the poem for the first time after his brother's death, William Michael Rossetti changed the title to 'Afterwards'. One can only conjecture he did so because the actual title was both too prescient and, posthumously, contributed to what had by then become an indelible narrative, a narrative forever uncannily inscribed in advance in the title of this early manuscript work:

> She opened her moist crimson lips to sing;
> And from her throat that is so white and full
> The notes leaped like a fountain. A smooth lull

117

Was o'er my heart: as when a viol-string
Having been broken, and the first musical ring
Once over, – all the rest is but a dull
Crude dissonance Echoless jar, howe'er thou twist and pull
The sundered fragments. A most weary thing
It is within the perished heart to seek
Pain, and not find it; but a sort of pall
Like sleep upon the mind. A cold set plan
Of life then comes; and grief that is not weak
Because it hath no tears. Say, can'st thou call
This a life, friend, or this man a man.

Arguably we find woven here all the strands of preoccupation we have been tracing. The poem begins with an image of the female voice: the presence of musical notes likened to those of a 'fountain', in the midst of which the ruined or wasted 'heart' of the speaker cannot feel. Indeed, the inability of the poetic 'I' to 'find' conciliatory pain is figured as 'a sort of pall/ Like sleep upon the mind': a hesitant state of death in life, as signified by the mantle or shroud here. The figure of Echo emerges in a tangential relationship and thereby, indirectly, so too does Narcissus. The 'unburied' Death of the title, that sense of an 'unnatural' absence of closure together with a desire to retrieve from loss 'death' itself by rendering it 'unburied', resonates in the most fundamental rhetorical questions with which the poem ends: 'Say, can'st thou call/This a life, friend, or this man a man.'

Yet, additionally, in its focus upon death as 'unburied', an absence of that state of interment that normally precedes resurrection, the poem indirectly calls up a little known poem from the 'coffined book'; it survives in the form of one of three remaining mutilated leaves. Entitled 'Another Love', that title is clearly added in a different hand at the end, the poem is chillingly prescient in physically realizing the interchangeability of the visual and verbal that we have been exploring:

Of her I thou [ght w] ho now is g[one s]o far:
And, the th[ought] passing over [t]o fall thence
Was like [a fall] from spirit into sense
Or from the heaven of heavens to a ~~mere~~ sun and star.
None other than Love's self ordained the bar
'Twixt her and me; so that if, going hence,
I met her, it could only seem a dense

118

Film of the brain, – just nought, as phantoms are.
Now, when I passed your threshold, & came in,
And glanced where you were sitting & did see
Your tresses in these braids & your hands thus,
I knew that other figure, grieved and thin,
That seemed there, yea that was there, could not be,
Though like God's wrath it stood dividing us.[2]

The leaf of the manuscript is damaged at the top in two places such that the first three lines are literally punctured, some of their words obliterated, the act of reading hampered. The transcript supplies in square brackets (as shown above) possible substitutions for those obliterations but even as thus represented the additions can't help but signal the peculiar form of partial defacement undergone by the original.

No matter how one regards it, what becomes for Rossetti located in an aesthetic of resurrection, in the embodiment of the shade, is the very possibility of re-figuring those categories of the material and the immaterial, the corporeal and the spiritual, verbal and visual that the Pre-Raphaelites aspired to realize. Inspired by Ruskin's inimitable aesthetic project, and long enduring the break up of the original 'PRB', as captured in Christina Rossetti's sonnet with which we began, the Pre-Raphaelites generated new conceptual possibilities from the age-old sister arts of poetry and painting. That compelling and all-pervasive relation between image and text that we have traced throughout engenders many characteristic representations. Finally, however, what remains most striking in those visual and verbal figures of resurrection that haunt Rossetti, and an aesthetic of Pre-Raphaelitism more generally, is a lament for a painting and poetry that may somehow meet in what Pater described as an 'unutterable desire penetrating into the world of sleep, however "lead-bound"'.[3]

Notes

PREAMBLE

1. William Holman Hunt, Letter to J. E. Millais 16 March, 1854.

INTRODUCTION

1. Charlotte Higgins, 'Turner Masterpiece stays in Britain as Tate raises £4.95m in Five Weeks', *The Guardian*, Friday 2 March 2007.
2. Lionel Stevenson, *The Pre-Raphaelite Poets* (Chapel Hill: University of N. Carolina), 1972.
3. Elizabeth Helsinger, *Poetry and the Pre-Raphaelite Arts: Dante Gabriel Rossetti and William Morris* (New Haven and London: Yale University Press), 2008.
4. Charles Dickens, 'Old Lamps for New Ones', *Household Words*, vol. 1, issue 12, (15 June, 1850), 265–267.
5. Adam Parkes, 'A Sense of Justice: Whistler, Ruskin, James, Impressionism' *Victorian Studies* 42 no.4 (1999), 593–629, 594.
6. Ibid. Charles Dickens, 'Old Lamps for New Ones', *Household Words* 15 June 1850, vol.1, 265–67.
7. Turner, *Snow Storm – Steam Boat off a Harbour's Mouth...*, oil on canvas 1842, the Tate Gallery; Holman Hunt *The Hierling Shepherd* 1851–2, oil on canvas, Manchester City Art Galleries.
8. See Lindsay Smith, '"The Seed of the Flower": Photography and Pre-Raphaelitism', *Victorian Photography, Poetry and Painting: the Enigma of Visibility in Ruskin, Morris and the Pre-Raphaelites* (Cambridge: Cambridge University Press, 1995, chapter 3, 93–112.
9. Carol Christ, *The Finer Optic: The Aesthetic of Particularity in Victorian Poetry* (New Haven and London: Yale University Press), 1975.
10. Helen Rossetti Angeli, *Dante Gabriel Rossetti: His Friends and His Enemies* (1949), 92.
11. M.H. Spielman, *John Ruskin, A Sketch of His Life, His Work, and His Opinions with Personal Reminiscences* (London: Cassell, 1900), 670.

CHAPTER 1: ONE TINY CALF-BOUND VOLUME

1. Ruskin's marriage to Effie Gray was annulled in 1854 after six years on the grounds of non-consummation owing to Ruskin's 'incurable impotency', a charge he refuted. Effie famously went on to marry Millais the following year. Just as this 'sensationalist fact' has stuck to Ruskin so to D. G. Rossetti has the occasion of 'digging up' poems.
2. The volume was published as *Poems* (London 1870), re-issued in different format, London 1881.
3. This is Maggie Berg's description of Ruskin's view of Rossetti: 'John Ruskin's Definition of D. G. Rossetti's Art', *Victorian Poetry* 20, 3–4 (1982), 103–12.
4. On theories of ekphrasis, see in particular: James Heffernan, *Museum of Words* (Chicago: University of Chicago Press, 1993); 'Ekphrasis and representation', (*New Literary History*, 22 1991, 301–2); Murray Krieger, *Ekphrasis: The Illusion of the Natural Sign* (Baltimore: Johns Hopkins University Press, 1991); W. J. T. Mitchell, *Picture Theory: Essays on Verbal and Visual Representation* (Chicago: University of Chicago Press, 1994); *What Do Pictures Want? The Lives and Loves of Images* (Chicago: University of Chicago Press, 2005).

CHAPTER 2: SEVERAL DEAD WOMEN AND ONE DEAD MAN

1. John Everett Millais, *Ophelia*, 1851–2, oil on canvas, the Tate Gallery, London.
2. William Holman Hunt, *Rienzi Vowing to Obtain Justice for the Death of his Brother, slain in a skirmish between the Colonna and Orsino factions*, 1849, oil on canvas, private collection. Henry Wallis, *The Death of Chatterton*, 1855–6, oil on canvas, the Tate Gallery.
3. Theodore Watts-Dunton (ed.) *T. H. Ward, English Poets*, 4 vols., vol 3. In fact, during this period, Rossetti amassed a set of historical notes on Chatterton, becoming fascinated by the legends that had grown up around him following his untimely death. The final line of the sonnet: 'And love-dream of thine unrecorded face' is especially resonant in the light of this study for it returns us to a human face, to the plenitude of an imagined, for some remembered, face for which no likeness survives. Of course, in a period prior to photography there could only have existed a pictorial record or a plastic one in the form of a death mask; a photographic 'likeness' was not yet realizable. And yet the train of Rossetti's poetic thought here is fervently post-photographic; that which he laments is the

absence of a photographic likeness.

4. D. G. Rossetti, 'Thomas Chatterton', *Poems and Ballads* (London: F. S. Ellis, 1881).

5. Geoffrey Hemstedt, 'Painting and Illustration' in Laurence Lerner, (ed.) *The Victorians* (London: Methuen, 1978), 139–52.

6. As Lawrence Alfred Phillips points out in *A Mighty Mass of Brick and Smoke: Victorian and Edwardian Reproductions of London* (London and New York: Routledge, 1996), 26: Wallis' painting was first 'photographed by Charles Wright of Holborn who exhibited his *Chatterton* at the Photographic Society in February 1857'. However, the Dublin photographer James Robinson's stereo tableau photograph 'The Death of Chatterton' (1860), that recreated Wallis' painting, was considered to have infringed the copyright that Augustus Egg the purchaser had taken out in order to give himself exclusive rights to engraved copies.

7. John Ruskin, Letter to John James Ruskin, 6 July 1853, *Ruskin* XIII, xxiv.

8. Rose La Touche was the daughter of John La Touche (1814–1904) a wealthy Irish banker and devout evangelical and Maria La Touche (1824–1906) a writer. Ruskin met Rose in 1858 when her mother asked him to give her daughters drawing lessons. From that point, there developed a friendship with the family and Ruskin's intense and tortured relationship with the religiously devout Rose remained for him unresolved following her death in 1875. Ruskin had proposed to her at seventeen and she had told him she would give him her answer at twenty-one. When that time came, Rose postponed her answer and, in October 1870, her mother wrote to Effie Millais enquiring about the circumstances of the annulment. Effie Millais' answer, including the claim: 'from his peculiar nature he is utterly incapable of making a woman happy. He is quite unnatural and in that one thing all the rest is embraced' (James 255), ensured that Rose la Touche's parents would prevent the marriage.

9. Walter Benjamin, 'A Small History of Photography', *One Way Street and Other Writings* (London: Verso, 1985).

10. Elizabeth Barrett, Letter to Lady Mitford, 1843, quoted in Betty Miller, *Elizabeth Barrett to Miss Mitford* (London: John Murray, 1954): 'It is not merely the likeness which is precious in such cases – but the association and the sense of nearness involved in the thing [...] the fact of *the very shadow of the person* lying there fixed for ever.'

11. 'Portrait of Rose La Touche on her Deathbed' 1875 Pencil (Ruskin Library, University of Lancaster).

12. Ruskin to Francesca Alexander, *John Ruskin's Letters to Francesca, and Memoirs of the Alexanders*, L. G. Swett (ed.) (Boston: Lothrop, Lee and

Shepard, 1931) 118.

13. Ruskin, Letter to Effie Ruskin, 24 April 1849, William James, (ed.) *The Order of Release: The Story of Effie Gray and John Everett Millais told for the first time in their Unpublished Letters* (London: John Murray, 1947), 138. In a letter to his wife from Chamonix, 24 June 1849, from the same tour Ruskin writes: 'I have been thinking of you a great deal in my walks today [...] but when I am measuring or drawing mountains, I forget about myself and my wife both; if I did not I could not stop so long away from her: for I begin to wonder whether I am married at all, and to think of all my happy hours, and soft slumber in my dearest lady's arms, as a dream'. (James 145).

14. Vittore Carpaccio, 'The Dream of St Ursula' from the 'St Ursula Cycle' commissioned in 1489 by the Confraternity of St Ursula for their Scuola of SS Giovanni e Paolo. When Ruskin began studying the 'cycle' in 1876 it was hanging in an incomplete state and out of sequence in the Academia, Venice.

CHAPTER 3: *UT PICTURA POESIS*: EARLY PRE-RAPHAELITE POETRY AND THE CASE OF *THE GERM*

1. *The Germ: Thoughts towards Nature in Poetry, Literature, and Art* issues 1–2 (London: Aylott & Jones, 1850). After the first two numbers the title changed to: *Art and Poetry: Thoughts towards Nature Conducted principally by Artists.*

2. Henry Peach Robinson, 'Fading Away', 1858 (George Eastman House Collection, New York).

3. Hans-Georg Gadamer, 'Poetry and Mimesis' in *The Relevance of the Beautiful and Other Essays* (Cambridge: Cambridge University Press, 1986).

4. William Morris, *The Defence of Guenevere and Other Poems* (London: Bell and Daldy, 1858).

5. Thomas Maitland, 'The Fleshly School of Poetry' *Contemporary Review*, October 1871.

6. *The Germ: A Facsimile reprint of the literary organ of the Pre-Raphaelite Brotherhood, published in 1850 with an Introduction by William Michael Rossetti* (London: Elliot Stock, 1901), 21.

7. Walter Pater, *Appreciations with an Essay on Style* (1889) 238.

8. Jean Hagstrum, *The Sister Arts: the Tradition of Literary Pictorialism and English Poetry From Dryden to Gray* (Chicago: University of Chicago Press, 1958)

9. Horace, *Ars Poetica* (II. 361 ff).

10. David Marshall, 'Ut Pictura Poesis', *The Cambridge History of Literary Criticism: the Eighteenth Century*, eds. H.B. Nisbet and Claude Rawson (Cambridge: Cambridge University Press, 2005), 681.

11. James Heffernan, 'Ekphrasis and Representation', *New Literary History*, 22 (1991), 301–2.

12. *The Work of Dante Gabriel Rossetti* (London: Ellis, 1911), 606.

13. Leonardo da Vinci, *Paragone: A Companion to the Arts*, trans. Irma A. Richter (London: Oxford University Press, 1949), 49.

14. Heffernan, 'Ekphrasis and Representation'.

15. Stephen Bann, 'Postscript: Three Translators – Silhouette, Barante, Rossetti', *Twentieth Century Studies*, I September 1974, 86–101.

CHAPTER 4: DANTE GABRIEL ROSSETTI'S 'PAIRED WORKS'

1. Thomas Hall Caine, *Recollections of Rossetti* (London: Elliot Stock, 1882), 284.

2. See for example Margaret Reynolds, 'Speaking un-likeness: the double text in Christina Rossetti's "After Death" and "Remember"', *Textual Practice* 13, I (spring 1999), 25–41; Catherine Maxwell, 'The poetic context of Christina Rossetti's "After Death"', *English Studies* 76: 2 (1995), 145–50.

3. Richard Stein, 'Dante Gabriel Rossetti and the Problem of Poetic Form', *Studies in English Literature* 1500–1900, vol. 10, no. 4 (1970), 775–92, 775.

4. Algernon Swinburne, *Notes on the Royal Academy Exhibition* 1868, 49

5. Ibid.

6. W. M. Rossetti, *Dante Gabriel Rossetti as Designer and Writer* (London: Cassell and Company, 1889), 58.

CHAPTER 5: 'THE FLESHLY SCHOOL' CONTROVERSY

1. Thomas Maitland, (Robert Buchanan), 'The Fleshly School of Poetry', *The Contemporary Review*, vol. 18, (1871) 334–350.

2. D. G. Rossetti, 'The Stealthy School of Criticism', *The Athenaeum*, December 1871.

3. Andrea Rose, *The Germ: the Literary Magazine of the Pre-Raphaelites* (Ashmolean Museum, Oxford, 1979).

4. Swinburne, 'Notes on Poems and Reviews', 1866, *Swinburne Replies: Notes on Poems and Reviews, Under the Microscope, Dedicatory Epistle*, Clyde K. Hyder (ed.) (Syracuse: Syracuse University Press, 1966).

5. D. G. Rossetti, 'How They Met Themselves' (1851–64). See Virginia Surtees, *The Paintings and Drawings of Dante Gabriel Rossetti, A*

Catalogue Raisonné, vol.1 (Oxford: Oxford University Press, 1971), 74.

6. See Swinburne's review, 'Charles Baudelaire: *Les Fleurs du mal'* first published in the *Spectator* 6 September 1862, reprinted in Cyde K. Hyder (ed.) *Swinburne as Critic* (London and Boston: Routledge, 1972).
7. D.G. Rossetti, 'The Stealthy School of Criticism', 332–3.
8. Sir John Skelton, *The Table-Talk of Shirley: Reminiscences of and Letters From Fronde, Thackeray, Disraeli, Browning, Rossetti, Huxley, Tyndall and Others* (Edinburgh: W. Blackwood & Sons, 1895), 78.
9. John Morley, *Saturday Review* 22 (Aug. 4 1866) 145–47, rep. in *The Critical Heritage* Clyde K.Hyder (ed.) (London 1970), 19.
10. Ibid.
11. Swinburne, 'Notes on Poems and Reviews', C.K. Hyder, *Swinburne Replies: Notes on Poems and Reviews, Under the Microscope, Dedicatory Epistle* (Syracuse: Syracuse University Press, 1966), 18.
12. Ibid.
13. Stevenson, 216.
14. Ibid.
15. Catherine Maxwell, *Swinburne* (Tavistock: Northcote House, 2006).
16. Karen Alkalay-Gut, 232.
17. Gadamer, 54.
18. Buchanan, 'Review of Poems and Ballads', *The Athenaeum* 4 August 1866.
19. Ibid., 164–5.
20. Alkalay-Gut, 232.
21. Ibid., 233.
22. See Shelley, *The Witch of Atlas*, composed 1820, published in *Posthumous Poems*. ed. Mary Shelley 1824. Théophile Gautier, 'Contralto' one of eighteen poems originally published in *Emaux and Camées* (1852).
23. McGann, *Swinburne: an Experiment in Criticism* (Chicago and London: Chicago University Press, 1972), 34.
24. Catherine Maxwell, *The Female Sublime from Milton to Swinburne: Bearing Blindness* (Manchester: Manchester University Press, 2001).
25. Ibid.
26. Thais E. Morgan, 'Reimagining Masculinity in Victorian Criticism: Swinburne and Pater', *Victorian Studies* 36/3 (1993), 315–32.
27. W. J. Courthope, *The Quarterly Review* (January, 1872), 59–84, 71.
28. Buchanan, 165.
29. Solomon was arrested with George Roberts and charged with 'conspiracy to commit buggery' that carried a maximum charge of two years. As Catherine Maxwell notes, after being released on bail, Solomon 'got off with a fine and the obligation "to appear when called"', whereas his 'companion' a '60-year-old stableman' was

'sentenced to eighteen months hard labour'. (*Swinburne*, 132 n.22).

30. Solomon, quoted in Colin Cruise et al, *Love Revealed: Simeon Solomon and the Pre-Raphaelites* (London: Merret, Birmingham Museum and Art Gallery, 2005), 156.
31. Swinburne, 'Review of Solomon', *The Dark Blue* 1 July 1871, 574.
32. *The Illustrated London News* 6 February 1869, 135.
33. Cruise, 52–53.
34. Stephen Bann, *The True Vine: On Visual Representation and the Western Tradition* (Cambridge: Cambridge University Press, 1989), 23.

CHAPTER 6: DANTE'S *LA VITA NUOVA*

1. D. G .Rossetti, *The Vita Nuova*, in Jan Marsh, *Dante Gabriel Rossetti: Collected Writings* (Chicago: New Amsterdam Books, 2000), 76–128. Hereafter, cited in text as *VN* followed by page number.
2. D. G. Rossetti, 'Dante's Dream on the Day of the Death of Beatrice: 9th June 1290' [Flysheet printing 1881] cited in Virginia Surtees, *The Drawings and Paintings of Dante Gabriel Rossetti (1828–1882) A Catalogue Raisonné* (Oxford: Oxford University Press, 1971).
3. W. M. Rossetti, Diary 30 May 1877, cited in Marsh, 521.

CHAPTER 7: THE SHADE

1. Marsh, 460.
2. Swinburne, 'The Garden of Proserpine', 'Hymn to Proserpine', as Maxwell notes 'robustly laments the displacement of paganism and its untroubled pleasures by the austerities of Christianity' (*Swinburne*, 89).
3. Frederic Leighton, *Orpheus and Eurydice* (1864). Oil on canvas, private collection.
4. Frederic Leighton, *The Triumph of Music: Orpheus by the Power of his Art, Redeems his Wife from Hades* (1855–6).
5. George Frederic Watts, *Orpheus and Eurydice* (1869). There are eight different versions of the painting: three in public galleries including this version, City of Aberdeen Art Gallery and Museum.
6. The iconic quality of the work marks out the later evolution of the aesthetic of Pre-Raphaelitism in a form similar to that found in Solomon's work.
7. Jay Prosser, *Light in the Dark Room: Photography and Loss* (Minneapolis: University of Minnesota Press, 2005).
8. D. G. Rossetti, 'Orpheus and Eurydice' pencil drawing, 1875 (the

British Museum). See Virginia Surtees, *The Paintings and Drawings of Dante Gabriel Rossetti, A Catalogue Raisonné* (Oxford: Oxford University Press, 1971) vol.1, 141.

9. *The Eclogues, Georgics and Aeneid of Virgil*, trans. C. Day Lewis (Oxford: Oxford University Press, 1966) Book IV, lines 471–508.
10. G. F. Watts, *Love and Death* 1874–7, 168.
11. Watts, 1912.

AFTERTHOUGHT

1. 'Unburied Death' (1848) MS, The British Library, Ashley Library: catalogue number: B3870. See The Rossetti Archive: www.rossettiarchive.org/docs/16.1848.blms.radheader.html
2. There exists an earlier version of the poem from 1848, entitled 'One With Two Shades' that more obviously represents the speaker's encounter with two resurrected figures: MS corrected fair copy, Duke University Library, catalogue number: Rossetti writings xx1. See the Rossetti Archive: www.rossettiarchive.org/docs/16.1848.dukems.radheader.html
3. Walter Pater, *Appreciations, with an Essay on Style* (1889), 238.

Select Bibliography

Andres, Sophia, *The Pre-Raphaelite Art of the Victorian Novel: Narrative Challenges to Visual Gendered Boundaries* (Columbus: Ohio State University Press, 2005).

Armstrong, Isobel, *Victorian Poetry: Poetry, Poetics and Politics* (London: Routledge, 1993).

Bann, Stephen, 'Postscript: Three Translators – Silhouette, Barante, Rossetti', *Twentieth Century Studies*, 1 September 1974, 86–101.

Barnes, Rachel, *The Pre-Raphaelites and their World* (London: Tate Gallery, 1998).

Barringer, Tim, *The Pre-Raphaelites: Reading the Image* (London: Everyman, 1998).

Benjamin, Walter, 'A Small History of Photography', *One Way Street and Other Writings* (London: Verso,1985).

Bennett, M., *PRB, Millais, PRA*, exh. cat (Liverpool: Walker Art Gallery, 1967).

Birch, Dinah, *Ruskin on Turner* (London: Cassells, 1990).

———, *Ruskin and the Dawn of the Modern* (Oxford: Oxford University Press, 1999).

Blanchot, Maurice, *The Gaze of Orpheus and Other Literary Essays*, trans. Lydia Davis (New York: Station Hill Press, 1981).

Bristow, Joseph ed., *The Cambridge Companion to Victorian Poetry* (Cambridge: Cambridge University Press, 2000).

Bronfen, Elizabeth, *Over her Dead Body: Death, Femininity and the Aesthetic* (Manchester: Manchester University Press, 1992).

Bullen, J.B., *The Pre-Raphaelite Body: Fear and Desire in Painting, Poetry and Criticism* (Oxford: Oxford University Press, 1998)

Burke, Edmund, *A Philosophical Enquiry into the Origin of our Ideas of the Sublime and the Beautiful*, ed. James Boulton (South Bend, Indiana: University of Notre Dame Press, 1968).

Byerly, Alison, *Realism, Representation and the Arts in Nineteenth-Century Culture* (Cambridge: Cambridge University Press, 1997).

Caine, Thomas Hall, *Recollections of Rossetti* (London: Elliot Stock,1882).

Chapman, Alison, *The Afterlife of Christina Rossetti* (St Martins Press,

2000).

———, ed., *Victorian Women Poets* (English Association, 2003).

Christ, Carol, *The Finer Optic: The Aesthetic of Particularity in Victorian Poetry* (New Haven and London: Yale University Press, 1975).

Corbett, David Peters, *The World in Paint: Modern Art and Visibility in England 1848–1914* (Manchester: Manchester University Press, 2004).

Cruise, Colin *et al.*, *Love Revealed: Simeon Solomon and the Pre-Raphaelites* (London: Merret, Birmingham Museum and Art Gallery, 2005).

Dearden, J. S., 'The portraits of Rose La Touche', *Burlington Magazine* vol. cxx, no. 899, Feb. 1978, 92–6.

Dickens, Charles, 'Old Lamps for New Ones', *Household Words* 15 June 1850, vol.1, 265–67.

Doughty, O. and Wall J. R., eds., *The Letters of Dante Gabriel Rossetti*, 4 vols, (Oxford: 1965–1967).

Flint, Kate, *The Victorians and the Visual Imagination* (Cambridge: Cambridge University Press, 2000).

Fredeman, W. E., *Pre-Raphaelitism: A Bibliocritical Study* (Cambridge Mass.: Harvard Unversity Press, 1995).

Gadamer, Hans-Georg, 'Poetry and Mimesis', in *The Relevance of the Beautiful and Other Essays* (Cambridge: Cambridge University Press, 1986).

Giles, Richard, 'The House of Life: A Pre-Raphaelite Philosophy' *Journal of Pre-Raphaelite and Aesthetic Studies* 2 (May 1982).

Gosse, Edmund, *The Life of Algernon Charles Swinburne* (London: Macmillan, 1917).

Hagstrum, Jean, *The Sister Arts: the Tradition of Literary Pictorialism and English Poetry From Dryden to Gray* (Chicago: U. of Chicago Press, 1958).

Harding, Ellen, ed., 'Re-Framing the Pre-Raphaelites', *Historical and Theoretical Essays* (Brookfield: Ashgate, 1996).

Hares-Stryker, C. ed., *An Anthology of Pre-Raphaelite Writings* (Sheffield: Academic Press, 1997).

Harrison, A.H., *Christina Rossetti in Context* (Charlotte: University of N. Carolina Press, 1988).

———, guest editor, *Centennial of Christina Rossetti 1830–1894, Victorian Poetry*, vol. 32, 3–4 (autumn-winter 1994), 201–511.

Heffernan, James, 'Ekphrasis and Representation', *New Literary History*, 22 (1991), 301–2.

———, *Museum of Words* (Chicago: University of Chicago Press, 1993).

Helsinger, Elizabeth, *Poetry and the Pre-Raphaelite Arts Dante Gabriel Rossetti and William Morris* (New Haven and London: Yale University Press, 2008).

Hewison, Robert, *John Ruskin: the Argument of the Eye* (Princeton:

Princeton University Press, 1976).

Hilton, Tim, *The Pre-Raphaelites* (London: Thames and Hudson, 1970).

Hollander, John, *Vision and Resonance: Two Senses of Poetic Form* (New Haven: Yale University Press, 1985).

———, *The Work of Poetry* (New York: Columbia University Press, 1989).

Holman Hunt, William, *Pre-Raphaelitism and the Pre-Raphaelite Brotherhood*, 2 vols. (London: Macmillan, 1905).

Hough, Graham, *The Last Romantics* (New York: Barnes and Noble, 1947).

Hunt, John Dixon, 'Ut Pictura Poesis, "the Picturesque", and John Ruskin', *Modern Language Notes* 93, 1978, 794–818.

Hutton, Richard Holt, 'Modern Poetry Microscopic', *North British Review* 28, February – May 1858.

Hyder, Clyde K. ed., *Swinburne: the Critical Heritage* (London: Routledge, 1970).

James, William, ed., *The Order of Release: The Story of Effie Gray and John Everett Millais told for the first time in their Unpublished Letters* (London: John Murray, 1947).

Krieger, Murray, *Ekphrasis: The Illusion of the Natural Sign* (Baltimore: Johns Hopkins University Press, 1991).

Landow, George P., *The Aesthetic and Critical Theories of John Ruskin* (Princeton: Princeton University Press, 1971).

Lang, Cecil Y. ed. *The Swinburne Letters* (New Haven: Yale University Press, 1959–62).

Lerner, Laurence, ed. *The Victorians* (London: Methuen, 1978).

Lessing, Gotthold Ephraim, *Laocoon: An Essay on the Limits of Painting and Poetry*, trans. Edward Allen McCormick (Baltimore: Johns Hopkins University Press, 1962).

Macleod, Dianne Sachko, *Art and the Victorian Middle Class* (Cambridge: Cambridge University Press, 1998).

Mancoff, Debra N., *John Everett Millais beyond the Pre-Raphaelite Brotherhood* (New Haven: Yale University Press, 2001).

Marsh, Jan, *Elizabeth Siddal 1829–1862: Pre-Raphaelite Artist*, exh. cat (Sheffield: Ruskin Gallery, 1991).

———, *Dante Gabriel Rossetti Painter and Poet* (London: Weidenfeld & Nicolson, 1999).

Marshall, David, 'Ut Pictura Poesis' in Nisbet, H. B. and Rawson, Claude (eds.) *The Cambridge History of Literary Criticism* (Cambridge: Cambridge University Press, 2005).

Matthews, Samantha, *Poetical Remains: Poets' Graves, Books and Bodies in the Nineteenth Century* (Oxford: Oxford University Press, 2004).

Maxwell, Catherine, 'The poetic context of Christina Rossetti's "After Death"', *English Studies* 76: 2 (1995), 145–50.

———, *The Female Sublime from Milton to Swinburne: Bearing Blindness*

(Manchester: Manchester University Press, 2001).

———, *Swinburne* (Tavistock: Northcote House, 2006).

McGann, Jerome, *Swinburne: an Experiment in Criticism* (Chicago and London: Chicago University Press, 1972).

———, *Rossetti Archive*, The Complete Writings and Pictures of Dante Gabriel Rossetti; a hypermedia Archive, http://www.rossettiarchive.org (2000), http://www.rossettiarchive.org/racs/doubleworks.rac.html

———, *Dante Gabriel Rossetti and the Game that Must Be Lost* (New Haven, Conn.: Yale University Press, 2000).

Michie, Helena, *Victorian Honeymoons: Journeys to the Conjugal* (Cambridge: Cambridge University Press, 2006).

Millais, John Guille, *The Life and Letters of John Everett Millais* 2 vols. (London: Macmillan, 1899).

Mitchell. W. J. T., 'Ekphrasis and the Other' *South Atlantic Quarterly* 1991 (summer 1992).

———, *Picture Theory: Essays on Verbal and Visual Representation* (Chicago: University of Chicago Press, 1994); *What Do Pictures Want? The Lives and Loves of Images* (Chicago: University of Chicago Press, 2005).

Morgan, Thais E., 'Reimagining Masculinity in Victorian Criticism: Swinburne and Pater', *Victorian Studies* 36/3 (1993), 315–32.

Myer, F. W. H. *Rossetti and the Religion of Beauty* (1983).

Parkes, Adam, 'A Sense of Justice: Whistler, Ruskin, James, Impressionism' *Victorian Studies* 42 no.4 (1999) 593–629

Parrish, L, ed., *Pre-Raphaelite Papers* (London: Tate Gallery, 1984)

———, *The Pre-Raphaelites*, exh. cat. Tate Gallery, 1984.

Pater, Walter, *Appreciations, with an Essay on Style* (London: Macmillan 1889).

———, *The Renaissance: Studies in Art and Poetry* ed. Donald Hill (Berkeley: University of California Press, 1900).

Phillips, Lawrence Alfred, *A Mighty Mass of Brick and Smoke: Victorian and Edwardian Reproductions of London* (London and New York: Routledge, 1996).

Pointon, Marcia, *Pre-Raphaelites Re-Viewed* (Manchester: Manchester University Press, 1989).

Praz, Mario, *Mnemosyne: the Parallel between Literature and the Visual Arts* (Princeton: Princeton University Press, 1970).

Prettejohn, E., *Art for Art's Sake: Aestheticism in Victorian Painting* (New Haven: Yale University Press, 2008).

———, *Art of the Pre-Raphaelites*, (London: Tate Gallery, 2000).

———, *Rossetti and his Circle* (New York: Stewart, Tabori and Chang, 1998).

Prosser, Jay, *Light in the Dark Room: Photography and Loss* (Minneapolis:

University of Minnesota Press, 2005).

Reid, David. G, ed., *Critical Essays on Dante Gabriel Rossetti* (New York: Macmillan, 1972).

Reynolds, Margaret, 'Speaking un-likeness: the double text in Christina Rossetti's "After Death" and "Remember"' *Textual Practice* 13, I (spring 1999), 25–41.

Rooksby, Rikky, *A.C. Swinburne: A Poet's Life* (Aldershot: Scolar Press, 1997).

———, and Shrimpton, N., eds., *The Whole Music of Passion: New Essays on Swinburne* (Aldershot: Scolar Press, 1993).

Rose, Andrea, *The Germ: the Literary Magazine of the Pre-Raphaelites* (Oxford: Ashmolean Museum, 1979).

Rosemblum, D., *Christina Rossetti: the Poetry of Endurance* (Carbondale Il: Southern Illinois Press, 1986).

Rossetti Angeli, Helen, *Dante Gabriel Rossetti: His Friends and His Enemies* (London: H. Hamilton, 1949).

Rossetti, D. G., *Family Letters with a Memoir by W. M. Rossetti* (London: Ellis and Elvey, 1895).

Rossetti, W. M. *Pre-Raphaelite Diaries and Letters* (London: Hurst and Blackett, 1900).

——— ed. *Ruskin: Rossetti: Pre-Raphaelitism Papers 1854–1862* (London: G. Allen, 1899).

——— 'The Royal Academy Exhibition' *Fraser's Magazine* 71 (June 1865).

Ruskin, John, *The Complete Works of John Ruskin* (library edition), ed. E. T. Cook and Alexander Wedderburn, 39 vols. (London: George Allen, 1903–12).

Sambrook, J., ed., *Pre-Raphaelitism: A Collection of Critical Essays* (London: University of Chicago Press, 1974).

Scott, William Bell, *Autobiographical Notes* ed. W. Minto. 2 vols. (New York, 1892).

Shaw, David W., *The Lucid Veil: Poetic Truth in the Victorian Age* (Madison: University of Wisconsin Press, 1987).

Smith, Lindsay, *Victorian Photography, Poetry and Painting: the Enigma of Visibility in Ruskin, Morris and the Pre-Raphaelites* (Cambridge: Cambridge University Press, 1995).

———, *The Politics of Focus: Women, Children and Nineteenth Century Photography* (Manchester: Manchester University Press, 1998).

Stanford, D., *Pre-Raphaelite Writing: an Anthology* (London: Dent, 1973).

Stein, Richard L., *The Ritual of Interpretation: the Fine Arts as Literature in Ruskin, Rossetti and Pater* (Cambridge, Mass: Harvard University Press, 1975).

———, 'Dante Gabriel Rossetti and the Problem of Poetic Form', *Studies in English Literature 1500–1900*, vol. 10, no.4 (1970), 775–92.

Stevenson, Lionel, *The Pre-Raphaelite Poets* (Chapel Hill: University of N.

Carolina Press, 1972).

Surtees, Virginia, *The Paintings and Drawings of Dante Gabriel Rossetti, A Catalogue Raisonne* (Oxford: Oxford University Press, 1971).

Swett, L. G., ed., *John Ruskin's Letters to Francesca, and Memoirs of the Alexanders*, (Boston: Mass., 1931).

Swinburne, A. C., *Poems*, 6 vols. (London: Chatto & Windus, 1905).

Warner, M., *et al.*, *The Pre-Raphaelites in Context* (San Marino, California: Henry E. Huntington Library, 1992).

Watts, G. E., *The Works of G. F. Watts*, RA exh. cat., New Gallery, London 1896.

Wildman, S., *Visions of Love and Life: Pre-Raphaelite Art from Birmingham Museums and Art Gallery* (Alexandria: Virginia: Art Services International, 1995).

Wilton, A. and Upstone, R. eds. *The Age of Rossetti, Burne-Jones and Watts: Symbolism in Britain*, exh. cat. (London: Tate Gallery, 1997).

Index

Alexander, Francesca 41, 122 n.12
Alkalay-Gut, Karen 84, 86, 125
    n.16
Alleyn, Ellen 47
Andromeda 73
Aristotle 61
Armstrong, Isobel 48, 55, 65, 104
Arnold, Matthew 80, 87
Athenaeum, The 71, 79

Bann, Stephen 64, 92, 124 n.15,
    126 n.34
Barrett, Elizabeth 40, 122n. 10
Barthes, Roland 110–11
Baudelaire, Charles 13, 17, 79, 92,
    125 n.6
Beatrice 23, 42, 43, 53, 69, 94–100
Benjamin, Walter 40, 122 n.9
Berg, Maggie 121 n.3
Blake, William 69
Blanchot, Maurice 68, 107–8, 110
Boccaccio 60
botanizing 20–5
Boyce, George P. 60
Brett, John *The Stone Breaker*, 16
Bronfen, Elizabeth 42–3, 108
Brown, Ford Madox *Pretty Baa
    Lambs*, 16, 26, 27
Browning, Robert 59, 80, 83, 104,
    107–8, 110, 114
Bruce, Henry 27
Buchanan, Robert 52–3, 'the

Fleshly School of Poetry'
    74–82, 85–6, 90, 125 n.18
Burke, Edmund 43
Burne-Jones, Edward 76

Carpaccio, Vittore 42, 123 n.14
Chatterton, Thomas 34, 36, 38,
    40, 117, 121 n.3
Christ, Carol 20, 120 n.9
Collins, Charles *Convent
    Thoughts*, 5
Collinson, Charles 5
Cook, E. T. 11
Cornforth, Fanny 23–4
Cornhill Magazine, The 13
Cruise, Colin 126 n.33

Dante, Alighieri 23, 42, 43, 65, 69,
    93, 100, 107–8, *Vita Nuova*,
    94–8
Dark Blue, The 91
Dickens, Charles 8, 15, 120 n.4
doubling 78
Dryden 61
Dudley Gallery 91
Durer, Albert 5

Egg, Augustus 122 n.6
Ekphrasis 33, 62, 65, 71–3, 90, 92,
    104, 107
Eurydice 72, 73–4, 87

Fine Art Society 39
Fry, Clarence 71

Gadamer, Hans-Georg 49, 62, 84,
    123 n.3, 125 n.17
Gautier, Théophile 86–7, 125 n.22
Germ, The 7, 45–57, 60, 70, 76, 123
    n.1
Graham, William 98
Gray, Euphemia Chalmers,
    (Effie) 28, 39, 40, 41, 61, 121
    n.1
Grosvenor Gallery 12
Guardian, The 4

Hades 101, 112, 114
Hagstrum, Jean 60, 123 n.8
Hazlitt, William 15
Heaton, Ellen 98
Heffernan, James 62, 64, 124 n.11
Hellenism 87
Helsinger, Elizabeth K. 7, 120 n.3
Hemstedt, Geoffrey 36, 122 n.5
hermaphrodite 33, 44, 62–3, 75–7,
    79, 89, 92
Highgate Cemetery 26–7
Higgins, Charlotte 120 n.1
Hollyer, Frederick 90
Horace 61, 64, 123 n.9
Hotten, John Camden 84
Howell, Charles Augustus 26
Hugo, Victor 13, 17
Hunt, William Holman 1, 2, 5, 8,
    10, 13, 15, 16, WORKS: *A
    Converted British Family
    Sheltering a Christian
    Missionary from the Persecution
    of the Druids*, 8, *The Hierling
    Shepherd*, 18, 38; *The Light of
    the World*, 19, 22; *Rienzi*, 8;
    The Scapegoat, 20, 22; 25, 34,
    38
Hyder, Clyde K. 124 n.4

Illustrated London News, The 126
    n.32

Keats, John 64, 86
Kreiger, Murray 121 n.4

La Touche, Rose 24, 39, 40–2, 122
    n.8
Leighton, Frederic *Orpheus and
    Eurydice* 106, plate 4, 107,
    108, 110, 126 n.3, 4
Leonardo Da Vinci 63, 124 n.12
Leyland, F. R. 91
Lytton, Edward Bulwer 8

Maitland, Thomas (Robert
    Buchanan) 75
Mallarmé, Stéphane 62
Manchester Art Treasures
    Exhibition 36
Marsh, Jan 27, 28, 29, 75
Marshall, David 61, 124 n.10
Marx, Karl 13
Mathews, C. P. 72
Maxwell, Catherine 88–9, 125
    n.24, 29, 126 n.2
McGann, Jerome 69, 73, 87, 125
    n.3
Medusa 72–3
Meredith, George 36
Michie, Helena 41
Millais, John Everett 1, 2, 8, 14,
    15, 16, 25, 34, 35, 36, 38, 39,
    40. WORKS: *Mariana*, 5,
    *Christ in the House of his
    Parents; 8, 16; John Ruskin,
    38–40; Ophelia*, 34, 35, plate 1,
    36–39; *The Return of the Dove
    to the Ark*, 9
Mitchell, W. J. T. 121 n.4
Morgan, Thais E. 89, 125 n.26
Morley, John 80, 82–3
Morris, Jane 101
Morris, William 7, 52, 75, 76, 81,

82, 90, 101, 123 n.4
Moxon, Edward 84

National Gallery of Melbourne 4

Ophelia 31, 33
Orpheus 73–4, 87, 105
Ovid 112

Parkes, Adam 12–13
Pater, Walter 2, 58, 89, 90, 115, 119, 123 n.7, 127 n.3
Perseus 73
Petrarch 97
photography 36, 38, 40, 46–7, 59, 74, 90, 121 n.3, 122 n.6
physiology of vision 18–20
Plato 61, 105
plein air painting 15, 38
Plutarch 61
Pluto 101
Poe, Edgar Allan 42, 65
Pre-Raphaelites 1–3, 5–7, 8–11, 13–17, 26–7, 32–3, 43, 46–65, 74, 75, 77, 81, 82, 85, 90, 94, 119; Pre-Raphaelite aesthetic 1, 6, 14, 16, 28, 33, 47, 101; brotherhood 1–3; colour in 15, 17, 85; empirical and transcendental in 16; phenomenon of presence 36, 38; realism 22, 40; and symbolism 20–1; 'truth to nature' 14; and Turner 17–20; vision in 15–16, 17–20; visual and verbal 1, 3, 24, 39, 44, 45, 85, 119; and ut pictura poesis 1, 11, 60–4, 76, 78, 80, 97, 114–15

Proserpine 69, 101–5, 107–8, 111, 114, 117
Prosser, Jay 110, 126 n.7
Proust, Marcel 5

physiology of vision 18

Quarterly Review, The 89, 125 n.27

Raphael 17
Reynolds, Joshua 15
Reynolds, Margaret 124 n.2
Rickards, Charles 114
Robinson, Henry Peach 46, 47, 123 n.2
Robinson, James 38, 122 n.6
Rose, Andrea 76, 124 n.3
Rossetti, Christina Georgina, 1, 2–3, 10, 43, 46, 47, 48–51, 53–8, 60, 67–8, 89, 117, 119; WORKS: 'A Pause of Thought' 54–6; 'After Death' 46; 'An End' 53–4; 'Dream Land' 48–51; Goblin Market and Other Poems 67; 'In an Artist's Studio' 57–8; 'PRB' 2–3, 119; 'Song' 56–7
Rossetti, Dante Gabriel 1, 2, 3, 5, 7, 8, 10, 14, 15, 17, 20–5; disinterment of poems 26–33, 36, 39, 40, 43, 45–7, 49–52, 57–64, 65–74, 75–82, 91–3, Vita Nuova 94–9, 100–12, 114, 117, 119, POEMS: 'A last Confession' 80; 'The Blessed Damozel' 45, 65–7; Dante at Verona and Other Poems 26; 'The Honeysuckle' 22–3; 'Jenny' 29, 78, 79; 'My Sister's Sleep' 45–7; 'The Portrait', 'Proserpina' 104; 'Sister Helen' 78; 'The Stealthy School of Criticism' 75, 79–80; The House of Life 68, 70; 'The Kiss' 105; Towards the House of Life 29; 'Unburied Death 117–18; Venus Verticordia 70-71; 'Willowwood' 58; 'The

Woodspurge' 20–1,
PAINTINGS: *Aspecta Medusa*
72–3; *Astarte Syrica* 71; *Beata
Beatrix* 100; *The Blue Bower*
17; *Bocca Baciata* 59, 97;
*Dante's Dream of the Death of
Beatrice* 98; *Fazio's Mistress* 59;
The Girlhood of Mary Virgin 8;
How They Met Themselves
71–2, 78; *Lady Lileth* 59;
Proserpine 69, 102, plate 3;
Regina Cordium 59; *Venus
Verticordia* 21, 23–5;
Rossetti, William Michael 2, 3, 5,
10, 26, 31, 45, 46, 49, 54, 56,
72, 98, 117
Rossetti Angeli, Helen 120 n.10
Royal Academy, The 14–15
Ruskin, John 1, 2, 4–25, 26, 28,
30, 34, 38–42, 45, 74, 76, 83,
103, 119, and Turner, 4–5,
8–10, 12. WORKS: *Academy
Notes* 9; *Diaries*, 4; 'Letter to
the Times 13 May 1851' 5;
Modern Painters I 15; *Modern
Painters* II 10, 14; *Modern
Painters* III 20–1; 'Rose La
Touche on her Death Bed'
40–1; *Praeterita*, 7; Pre-
Raphaelitism 9, 17–18; *The
Stones of Venice* 13; *Unto This
Last* 13

Sappho 79
Saturday Review, The 82
Shakespeare, *Hamlet* 34
Shelley, Percy 64, 86, 125 n.22
Siddal, Elizabeth Eleanor 7, 22,
23, 24, exhumation 26–33, 39,
100, 111
Sidney, Philip 51
Skelton, John 125 n.8
Smith, Lindsay 7, 59
Solomon, Simeon 1, 43, 64, 75,

89, 'Sacramentum Amoris'
90–2, 95, 101, 110, 116, 125
n.29, 126 n.30
Spielman, M. H. 120 n.11
Stein, Richard 70, 124 n.3
Stephens, Frederic George 2, 3,
5, 103
Stevenson, Lionel, 7, 83
Surtees, Virginia, 126 n.2, 127 n.8
Swinburne, Algernon Charles 1,
13, 30, 31, 33, 43–4, 64, 71, 75,
77, 79–80, 91, 94, 95, 101,
'Anactoria' 84; 'Delores' 86;
'Hermaphroditus' 86–9; 'The
Garden of Proserpine' 104–5';
Poems and Ballads 82–90;
Songs Before Sunrise 112, 114,
115–16

Tate Britain 4
Tebbs, H.V. 26
Tennyson, Alfred 6, 46, 49, 50,
66, 80, 83, 104
Times, The 5, 8, 15
Trevelyan, Lady 83
Turner, Joseph Mallard William
4, 5, 8, 9, 10, 14, 17, 18, 19;
WORKS: *The Blue Rigi* 4, *The
Dark Rigi* 4, *The Red Rigi* 4,
*Snow Storm – Steam Boat off a
Harbour's Mouth* 18–19

Ut pictura poesis 1, 11, 60–4, 76,
78, 80, 97, 114–15

Virgil 112–14

Wallis, Henry *The Death of
Chatterton* 34, 36, 37, plate 2,
38, 39, 40, 81
Ward, T. H. 36
Waterhouse, William 6
Watts, George Frederic *Orpheus
and Eurydice* 109, plate 5, 110;

Love and Death 114–15, 126 n.5

Watts-Dunton, Theodore, 36

Wedderburn, Alexander 11

Whistler, James McNeil 12–13, 86

Wilde, Oscar 2, 38

Williams, Dr. Llewellyn 26, 28

Woolner, Thomas 2, 5, 'Of My lady in Death' 51–2

Printed and bound by CPI Group (UK) Ltd, Croydon, CR0 4YY

13/04/2025

14656585-0001